First published by Rosie Shilo, 2018

© Rosie Shilo 2018

www.virtuallyyours.com.au

Title: Reaching for the Stars: A woman's guide to becoming a Stellar Virtual Assistant / Rosie Shilo.

ISBN: 9780646992655 (paperback)

Book cover design and layout by eMatti

Printed and distributed in Australia by IngramSpark

Keywords:
     Virtual Assistant
     VA
     Virtually Yours
     Rosie Shilo
     Virtual network
     Virtual training network

DISCLAIMER

You should always seek independent financial advice and thoroughly read terms and conditions relating to any insurance, tax, legal, or financial issue, service, or product. This book is intended as a guide only.

REACHING

FOR THE

STARS

A woman's guide
to becoming a
Stellar Virtual Assistant

ROSIE SHILO

FOUNDER OF THE VIRTUALLY YOURS
VIRTUAL ASSISTANT & TRAINING NETWORK

To my two beautiful daughters,
Ruby and Ella – may the world of opportunities
be yours for the taking, now and for always.
You light up my life.

ACKNOWLEDGEMENTS

This book, my business, my previous book and my amazing lifestyle are all thanks to some very key people in my world, who are always there to motivate me, inspire me, lend an ear and to keep it fun.

Firstly, my husband, Greg. My rock. Who else would live with me for so long, work from home with me and raise my girls with me and not run screaming for the hills?

My girls, Ruby and Ella, who are why I wanted to work from home in the first place. They were the best reason then and still are today.

My Dad, for always believing in me and giving me the confidence to do what I want - you've been incredible.

My gorgeous Hannah. Where have you been all my life? My kindred spirit – which is scary, because you're kinda bonkers.

My incredible Mon. The most reliable and wonderful person I have ever worked with and have had the joy of becoming dear friends with. This book could only have happened with the knowledge in my head and heart that you'd be there backing me, checking for errors, and making me sound smarter than I probably am.

To Kym and Korryn – thank you both so much for your eagle eyes and fabulous proofreading support.

To Evelyne, who has given so much time and energy to turn my words into a visual beauty – you are an angel a very special part of my biz journey.

To Jemma and Anita for sharing their onboarding forms with us. To Kristie, Birgit, Susie, Hanna, Rachel A, Sarah, Julieanne, Stacey, Kristy and Rachel B for sharing your VA experiences with us all. Your words, along with Evelyne and Monique, will no doubt ease the minds of many new VAs.

To Gary Horsman for his fantastic professional contribution around business insurance, and Christie Mims for her tips on finding your skills and talents.

To Sophie Timothy for my super fun cover photos!

To my best friends, you know who you are. You've been there with me along this life journey for so long and always always supported my desire to work for myself and to have an impact on the VA Industry.

To my VYVA members. YOU are what keeps me going in business day in and day out. You'll never know the joy you bring into my world. I'm so glad you value what I offer and that you are doing such wonderful things for women in business and for the VA Industry as a whole.

CONTENTS

PREFACE

About this book

This book supports VAs through all stages of their business.

On the one hand, you may have recently decided that it's time you became your own boss. You're sick of the rat-race, reporting to a boss and being a small cog in someone else's grand scheme.

Many new VAs are full-time mums, determined to get back into the swing of things, but on your terms. This could be daunting too as you may have been out of the 'game' for a few years and not sure if your skills are up to scratch.

On the other hand, you may already be a VA. You've been going for a few years, but there are a couple of things that are stopping you or slowing you down from reaching your absolute goals. You need to regroup.

In this book, we'll look at some of the hurdles that VAs often face as they're setting up, and after they've set up the basics of their business.

We'll explore the basic setup processes and work through to higher level business blocks. By the end of this book, you'll know how to set up your business, work out your ideal client, ensure your structures are strong and be working smarter, not harder.

If you've been in business a few years already, you may find that some of the areas we explore in this book, you've already worked through. However, we hope that you find each area gives you at least one 'takeaway' that you can consider for your business and utilise to succeed further and meet your goals.

My name is Rosie Shilo, and I'm the owner of Virtually Yours, a highly respected Virtual Assistance and Training Network in Australia, established in 2004.

I've supported thousands of Virtual Assistants through the start-up phase of their business and cheered them on as their businesses grew and succeeded. I've supported those who faced moments of uncertainty, those who questioned themselves, those who faced issues within their businesses, and those who wanted someone to listen to a new idea or project. And I've learnt so much along the way.

I've been asked the same questions again and again, and that's what has inspired this book. Tapping into the minds of those who've gone before you can be very useful. You'll learn theories that work, along with hearing the stories of VAs just like you.

Being a Virtual Assistant makes you a business owner. You are no longer an employee. This means an entirely new mindset, new levels of responsibility, probably new tools and resources, and most importantly, unlimited opportunities.

Being virtual means facing unique hurdles. You'll be online most of the time and technology will be your friend and your foe. Social media is commonly used a lot, and this can be an arena that boosts your confidence and then pulls you down – sometimes in the same day.

As a business owner, you'll be told by others that your dream is one thing (6 or 7 figure business) when perhaps in reality, it's another; that you're failing if you're not doing what they tell you to do; that you're a fraud or not good enough. Knowing what your dreams are and staying true to those will be vital.

We will explore these further and arm you with the tools to avoid falling into self-sabotage.

Running a business is a crazy undertaking.
It's not easy – but it's worth it!

www.virtuallyyours.com.au

HOW I STARTED

***

I was 25 years old when I started my business.

I'd been working in the disability sector for a few years, and before that, I'd mainly had reception and office management type jobs. I loved the disability sector. It felt like home. The people made me laugh (and cry). My clients and their families were so beautiful and appreciative of all that was good in the world, even though they had more to deal with than most. We all worked tirelessly and the staff from other departments were so fun and welcoming when I'd visit their offices for a chat.

But over the years, I got more and more frustrated with the increasing limitations that were put on our team, with more and more expectations piled on top. Staff were getting angry and clients were getting frustrated. In the end, I was getting migraines so often that I stopped planning to attend any events on the weekend simply because I didn't know if I'd be functioning or not. There was simply too much conflict in a place that should have been all about supporting and caring for those in need. I ended up visiting a specialist for my migraines who told me to take two weeks off work and to start on some migraine management medication.

At that stage, I had moved back home with my Dad to regroup and build my health back up. Not only was I struggling with those migraines, but I had severe depression stemming from Post-Traumatic Stress. And even though the PTS had started about five years prior, I'd only just started to treat it. I was struggling to see a way forward and to work out how on earth I could hold down a job.

My Dad ran his own business from home, and it was great seeing the success he was achieving. It was Dad who suggested I could offer my administrative support to business owners like himself, who worked independently and didn't want to hire staff. I thought this was a great idea for a bit of a side-project. To be honest, I didn't see it as a potential career.

I hopped online, which back then was more like 'hiked online' as I had to make sure no-one was on the phone or my super slow dial-up connection would fail. Keeping my fingers crossed that the phone wouldn't ring and interrupt my connection, I started researching 'administration services' as a business model. I found the small, but evolving, Virtual Assistant world with people like Kathie Thomas and Anita Kilkenny leading the way.

My first few jobs were secured through Kathie's online network 'A Clayton's Secretary'. They were a massive learning curve. Even sending large files back then was a big deal and fraught with drama. It could take an hour to send a file and then you've got to hope they were able to download it at the other end. And then what if the file formatting changed from my computer to theirs? The words 'dog's dinner' always come to mind when I think about formatting after an incident where a thesis I formatted messed up in transit and the client used those words to describe it.

I quickly had to learn the more technical side to desktop publishing (Microsoft Publisher is NOT a publishing program!) and to create HTML websites. I got some things wrong, and I got other things right. And I kept on learning.

By this stage, probably six months after starting my venture, I'd decided to quit my job and focus on making this business work. I remember going in to work one day and seeing the mail still on the desk that I'd asked my co-worker to post on the day I don't work (by post, I mean drop in to reception upstairs). I was so frustrated because it was one of so many things she'd not done since she'd started working with me that I texted my partner (now husband) and asked, 'If I can't make enough money, will you still feed me?'. He said 'yes' so I wrote my resignation letter and took it to my manager that very day.

At home my Dad set up an office for me with its own phone line and I rounded up the basic equipment I needed such as a computer, desk, chair, phone and printer. I worked downstairs while Dad worked upstairs. At midday, we both stopped for lunch and watched TV in the kitchen while we ate and chatted. Usually something like 'All creatures great and small' or 'To the Manor Born' or 'Seinfeld' gave us a few laughs. It was such a lovely tradition. I remember each day Dad would say either 'Rose, no one loves me!' because he didn't have much work, or he'd say 'Rose, I have too much work!' because there was plenty. He'd laugh either way. When it was quiet he did his own thing on our large country property and appreciated the break. When he was busy he just worked hard. He always showed me that business came in flows and you just appreciated what it was at the time.

My background in the disability sector hadn't been a passing fancy. I've always had a desire to support and help others in any way I can. And I soon realised that I wanted to create a community for other Virtual Assistants. A place to connect, feel less isolated and collaborate. I also realised early on that many VAs would have started their businesses because they wanted to work around children and/or they had some kind of situation in their life that made employment more stressful – such as depression. I wanted to support them and allow that to support me in return. I definitely planned on having kids in the future and wanted to be able to be home for them.

But let me tell you, setting a network up wasn't easy. Social media barely existed (shock horror hey!) and MySpace was not for business! I couldn't create a Facebook group, use a few hashtags, create some ads and invite people to join me. Back then Facebook Pages didn't even exist yet. Nor did Twitter. And LinkedIn was only 2 years old and in its infancy.

For many years, I had to host my online community on a PHP forum on my website. It was clunky and not overly interactive as people just weren't online very often. And getting people to join a 'network' of one was no easy feat either! But I still managed to build it up into a respectable number.

My most successful strategy was to use Google to find other Virtual Assistants in Australia and ask them to complete a survey for me in return for one-year free membership to the Virtually Yours network. The survey asked them what they wanted from a network. It was great content for me to work from, and I was able to have, for one year at least, a larger group of people in my network.

Your network is only as good as the people in it, so building up the quantity and quality was important. My tactic worked! After their free year, many of those VAs stayed on and became financial members. And some of them are still on my network today!

Over the years I've tried all sorts of things to meet the needs of my members. I find out those needs simply by asking. And I ask all the time. Then I listen. I suggest. And I listen again.

Like most business owners, I've had periods of time where I've wanted to pack it all in. I nearly brought on a business partner at one stage, and at another stage, I almost sold the business outright. But I always found myself back in the driver's seat, and after a little time out, I feel reinvigorated to keep going and try new things.

I'm lucky that my hubby, kids, friends and family have always been supportive of my business ideas. I've never been told I should go and 'get a job'. I've had years where I barely made enough money to survive and some years where I did very well. I've had years where I worked way too many hours, and now I'm finally at a point where I work exactly the number of hours I want to.

Every single year I stuff something up. Something big – like accidently deleting all of my member subscriptions in one fell swoop. Every single year I learn something new. Every single year I try something new. Every single year I achieve great things.

I've been told by gurus and coaches over the years to charge more, to use offshore VAs as contractors and make a solid margin from that. I've read stories about what I should be if I want to succeed and realised that I'm just not that person – and accepted it. I've had years and years worth of self-doubt and imposter syndrome. I don't have some epic story I want to share about my disastrous life before success and I don't want to charge tens of thousands of dollars to VAs who want to create their own businesses. I don't claim to be a guru and I don't have all the answers. I don't want to build a VA team and manage them to support a bunch of clients. I hate doing transcription and I cannot be relied on to make any kind of cold-call. My follow ups are pretty pathetic, and I don't like to sell.

So, I just do my thing and I share. I share how much I love my VYVA community and the VA industry. I share what I learn with my members, so they can grow and build this community up even more.

I may not be a millionaire but damned if I'm not writing this book from a gorgeous café with a lovely biz friend across the table from me (Sam from Sam Says – love ya, hon!) working on her great VA biz while hubby wrangles my three year old while trying to do his work (good luck, babe!) and my eight year old is at school down the road. My life is pretty damn awesome. So, in my eyes, that's my definition of success. I hope you know what yours is.

I love my business. And these days, I can't imagine doing anything else. I have hobbies which are completely different from my business, such as gardening and painting murals on walls. People have suggested I turn my hobbies into businesses. But I think having hobbies, with no commitment to anyone, is important, so they'll stay as hobbies only. I call them my 'non-negotiables' and they are vital to my mental health. They are part of my mental health strategy.

My business team is the most important part of my business. My VA, Monique, my best friend and business-buddy Hannah, my husband Greg and the many other business women and men who I collaborate with, learn from, laugh with and share with are all that my business is founded on. Without them, I wouldn't even bother, to be honest.

I've always been as honest and genuine as possible in my business. Everyone knows who I am – I'm an open book. In person; I'm the same as I am online or in this book and you can like it or not – up to you! But because of this, I've attracted so many like-minded people into my world and that, to me, is why I love what I do so much.

So, I hope this book can give you some tips and resources, and inspire some new ideas and thinking to make your business something you love and want to do for a very long time!

xxx Rosie

WHAT IS VIRTUAL ASSISTANCE?

***

The Virtual Assistant industry includes a huge number of service providers who all have three things in common:

- They work offsite from their client and are therefore 'virtual',
- They provide business support services, and
- They are an independent contractor/self-employed, not an employee.

'Business services' is a huge industry. And thanks to modern technology, most business services can be provided virtually. Business services include administration, bookkeeping, graphic design, web design and maintenance, transcription, reception services, social media management, copywriting, and video editing just to name a few. We've included a comprehensive list at the end of this book. It's pretty long!

So, when people refer to the Virtual Assistant industry,

they are referring to all business support services which can be offered from offsite. And this is HUGE.

Many service providers don't work under the heading of 'Virtual Assistance' mainly because the term was coined before technology allowed for these higher-end services to be offered in this way. Many people still consider Virtual Assistance to be low-end administrative support – almost entry level in some cases. This is compounded by the fact that a lot of the cheaper offshore Virtual Assistant services offer the more basic administration services predominantly, and they are heavily promoted by certain coaches with large followings.

As people who have worked with EAs and PAs know, administration can be very complicated and time-consuming. There are a lot of VAs in Australia who are exceptionally skilled in administration. They've taken their experience and skills from working in employee roles and increased their knowledge and skill set by turning those skills into a professional business. So, for other business owners, this is even better – someone who is mad about admin AND knows what running a business is all about? Very useful indeed.

I find many people understand how big and generic the term Virtual Assistant is when I compare it to the Trades Industry. A plumber or an electrician have very different skill sets, solve very different problems and use very different tools. But they are both in the Trade Industry. You don't search for a plumber by Googling "Tradie" even though you know that they fall under this heading. It's just too broad. If you came across a tradesman who simply said that they were a "Tradie – I do everything!" wouldn't you find that a little confusing and unhelpful? What do they do? Are they a jack of all trades and a master of none?

In the same way, Virtual Assistants need to be more specific about what their actual service is and promote it accordingly.

Importantly, by restricting yourself to the title of Virtual Assistant and trying to cover the whole gamut of services within the industry, you're not going to be able to charge what you're worth. On the flip side, educating as many people as possible about the Virtual Assistant industry will help you and your peers. Please don't hide from the term – just educate people and be clear what your role in the Virtual Assistant Industry is.

VAs who do well in business usually specialise and niche. They focus their training, processes, marketing and energy on an area so that they can do it amazingly well. These VAs don't fear missing out on clients because of their niche – they know their ideal client and where they can find them. These VAs often partner with other VAs who offer complimentary business solutions and refer clients to them when necessary.

In a nutshell, a Virtual Assistant works within the Virtual

Assistant industry. They may be a bookkeeper, a business manager, a website developer or a copywriter (to name a few) but they are also an independent contractor who has clients, not employers. They work from their office location and provide the majority of their services virtually. They are their own boss. They can make their business anything they want.

VA Code of Ethics document https://www.virtuallyyours. com.au/wp-content/uploads/Core-Competencies-Second-Edition-061307.pdf.

There is a simple but useful document you should familiarise yourself with, called the VA Code of Ethics. It was created in 2007 by a group of VAs from an international board for the International Alliance of Virtual Business. The Alliance set up a core competency committee that worked on putting this document together to guide VAs everywhere on the basic ethical standards that you should always adhere to. This document is so relevant and has got some great points. It's essential for all VAs to read this.

FIVE KEY BENEFITS

***

This book is here to guide you through the various steps to building a successful VA business, or as I like to say, a Stellar VA Business!

There are five key benefits that you will receive from this book and the VA coaching programs run by Virtually Yours.

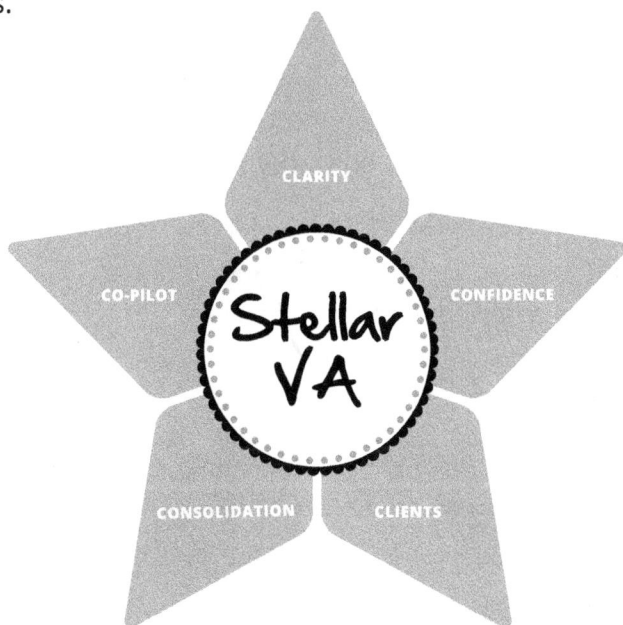

Clarity

One of the hardest things about running a successful business is gaining clarity on what you want to achieve and how you want to achieve it. Within that are questions around who you want to work with, what sort of skills you want to be providing, how you want to deliver the services and so on.

Without clarity, you can find yourself working on too much or too little, and all without a strong direction. I see this when people spend the first part of their business setup focusing on creating a logo, coming up with a name, getting the logo printed on shirts, getting branded stationery, business cards, domain names etc. All of this is needed of course, but when you spend all of your time focused on making the business 'look good' instead of building a structure that is strong, planned and researched, you find you end up with no money, no clients and still, no clarity. Therefore, working through clarity first is important.

When we look at clarity, we explore how you best function, what your end goal is, and importantly, whether or not you have what it takes to be a VA.

Confidence

Confidence is a significant part of running a business. You'll find your confidence can be challenged along the way, and although the challenges change over time, they won't necessarily ease up. So in this section, we explore what confidence looks like to you, the reality of what is happening around you and some experiences from other VAs who are running businesses just like yours.

Clients

Without being clear on what your skills are, what services can be created from those and who needs them, you won't find clients.

Not everyone knows what fabulous skills they have – so delving into what you have experience in, what you find yourself doing on autopilot and what excites you is not only interesting and fun, but it's hugely useful when creating the services around which you want to build your business.

Consolidation

There are a lot of things that need to be considered and set up behind the scenes to get your business running smoothly.

From marketing to communication, from pricing to insurances and even managing teams and time – all of this needs to be set up and planned properly if you want your business to thrive. Consolidation is a BIG area, and there are a lot of things you need to explore and tick off for your business – so make sure you have a pen and notebook with you when we work through this!

Co-pilot

Now, how lucky are you? Having a co-pilot along the ride to help you on this journey is a bonus. And while I'm only here within these lines at the moment, you are obtaining years and years of experience within one glorious book – saving you time, mistakes and uncertainty.

If you want more support in the form of a co-pilot, make sure you touch base with me, and we can explore your business growth together.

THE VIRTUAL ASSISTANT

✱✱✱

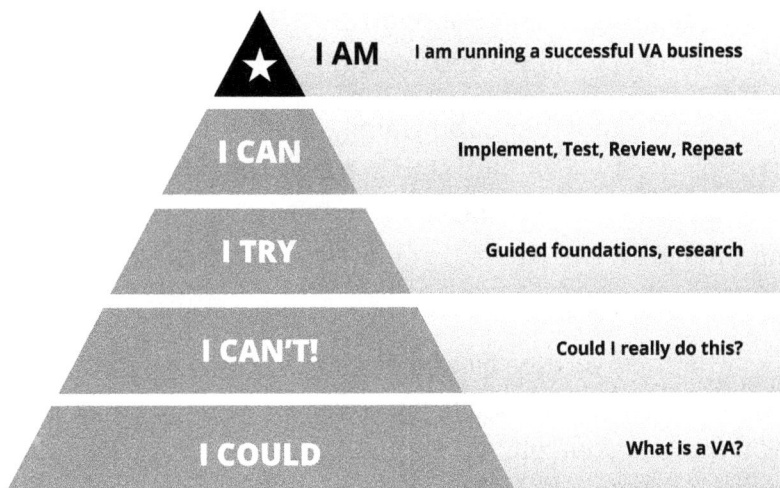

★	I AM	I am running a successful VA business
	I CAN	Implement, Test, Review, Repeat
	I TRY	Guided foundations, research
	I CAN'T!	Could I really do this?
	I COULD	What is a VA?

I could...

Over the years I've seen hundreds if not thousands of Virtual Assistants starting up their exciting new business. It's a really big step and a very thrilling one.

Often, the journey begins when someone says to you, 'Hey did you think of becoming a Virtual Assistant?' , or 'With those skills, you should become a Virtual Assistant'.

At the time you probably thought to yourself – umm, what the hell is a Virtual Assistant? Isn't that just a cartoon image of a person talking you through the help process on a website?

You start Googling and find that there is indeed a thriving industry of Virtual Assistants, all working from home, offering business support services to their wonderful clients, making money and living the dream!

You tell your friends and family (if you're brave enough!), 'I'm going to be a VA!' and start setting yourself up. You work on a biz name, service ideas, pricing, create a Facebook page and maybe a website and you even join a cool VA network like Virtually Yours.

But then you see all of the skills everyone else has. You see how much they know. You realise how little you know. You think to yourself...

I can't...

You wonder why you haven't got a bunch of clients yet. You wonder if you could deliver what they need. Maybe you've supported a client, and they were mean to you or asked you to do things outside of your normal hours, or maybe they didn't pay their invoice.

You look at the multitude of CRMs, social media platforms, editing programs, shortcuts, website plugins, and services all being provided by those other VAs who know so much and are doing so well. You wonder if maybe you should just quit while you're ahead. Maybe you should just get a regular job. Or maybe you could start working for less just to get the experience and just to get one client to jump on board...

Or perhaps you see all this but the drive is so strong in you, and you think to yourself, 'I'm doing this anyway! I'm going to make it work!'. You put your head down and your bum up, and you start to explore all of the areas you think you should be learning. You decided you can do this yourself and you will get there no matter what. And you think to yourself...

I try...

I will keep trying. I am the engine that could. I can do this.

You keep researching, and you learn by trial and error. Many errors. You offer a range of services and promote them to groups online. You respond to callouts for VAs from business owners in Facebook and let them know you can help. You promote your services – all of them – to everyone. It's slowly growing, but it's exhausting.

You think to yourself; I can go one of two ways. I can either keep exploring this on my own and slowly grow my business, or I can get some professional guidance and start working strategically. You find a great mentor who aligns with your values, and you have a chat with them about how they could help you move forward, and you realise...

I can...

With the support of a professional VA trainer, you start to research, test and implement. Then you review and repeat. You create strong foundations and automation to ensure you are working smarter, not harder. You get clear on your service offering and who the best clients are for you. You start kicking some serious goals. You know how to learn from what doesn't work. You move forward, and you gain confidence. You have clarity, clients, confidence and consolidation now that you are working with your co-pilot. And then you realise...

I am!

I am a stellar VA! I am running my dream biz. I am working with people who inspire and drive me, who challenge me in good ways and bring out the best in me. I am helping business owners achieve their goals through services I am passionate about. I am working the hours I want and making the money I want. I AM A STELLAR VA!

THE INGREDIENTS OF A STELLAR VA

✱✱✱

If you think about a successful VA – and we all know someone who we look at and think 'wow, they are rocking this VA thing' – what are the key areas you think that they have mastered to get there?

Here's what I think.

There are five areas you need to master to become a Stellar VA.

1. Skills

You need to have skills. This may seem like an obvious statement, however many people who can turn on a computer and check their emails or hang out on Facebook, think that they have 'skills'. And those are a couple of skills however they are not enough.

You need to have really strong skills in the area of service you wish to offer as well as understand all of the skills you need to deliver it. So perhaps you have great social media skills. You need to also understand marketing, audiences, design, communication, behind the scenes social media tech, managing a CRM and bookkeeping software and be able to represent yourself online and offline professionally.

2. Vision

A successful VA has a clear vision. They know why they are doing what they are doing (the Big Why) and they know what that vision will look and feel like when they achieve it. They let their vision guide them with business direction and business choices.

3. Mindset

A business mindset is quite different from an employee mindset. When you run a business with an employee mindset, you come into all sorts of trouble because the roles are very different and need to be treated as such. Simply because you work for your clients, doesn't mean you treat them like you did your manager or boss. You must run your business professionally and be a business owner at all times.

4. Process

A stellar VA has processes and procedures in place to ensure that their mission, service, communication and delivery are all consistent and professional. Clients need to feel confident and assured that they are getting a consistent service, based on what you have promised through your marketing and communication. With confusion or uncertainty comes unhappy clients and a stressed VA.

5. Communication

The best VAs have amazing communication skills. Your communication skills can make or break you. Over the years I have made heaps of communication mistakes, and they've always cost me at the time. But I do learn from them – so make sure you do too. Everything you say or write needs to be true, genuine and fair. You need to speak and write with your brand mouth and understand that this is what will attract or repel clients or associates.

Now that you know what you need to master to become a Stellar VA, let's explore each area in more detail. Throughout the rest of this book, we will be working through the 5 step process I take my VA clients through.

Let's get started!

YOU!

***

What is your end goal?

Knowing what you want to achieve in your business will help guide you with all decisions, clients, and projects you decide to take on. When we don't know exactly why we're

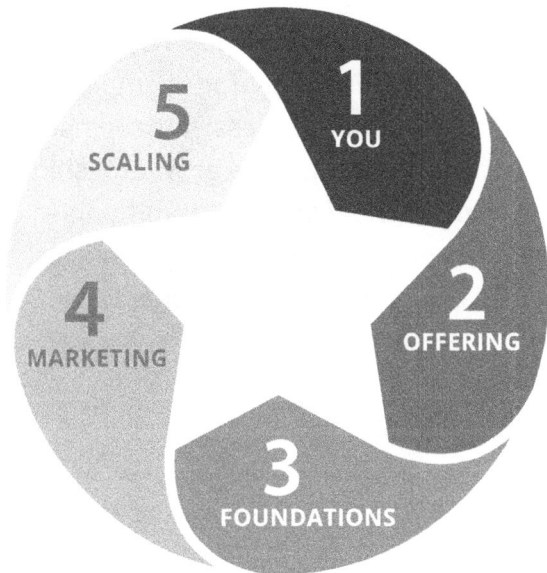

doing something and what the end goal looks like, we end up choosing randomly and often going off on tangents. I've been there. Especially if you're a bit of a 'magpie' like me, who likes shiny new things/ideas! Or on the opposite end, perhaps you find yourself getting too bogged down in the day to day and not coming up for fresh air and checking in on the bigger picture.

Your end goal may evolve but checking in to see if you are still connected is very important.

Often, when I ask people why they set up their VA business, they talk about being there for their kids or something along those lines. This is great and very important, however, what you may find is that your end goal is different to the benefit of working around the kids and bigger than the services you're offering.

You may find that your work has a bigger impact on the world than simply writing copy for example. Often Virtual Assistants (and women in business) find themselves pushed by the drive to help other people grow and shine, and that in turn, can impact whole families, communities or causes. My 'big why' for example, is to see the Australian Virtual Assistant industry grow to be a professional, skilled and valued industry so women who want to work around family or for themselves can do so. I want Virtual Assistants to feel respected and empowered and be able to charge what they're worth by delivering professional services. These women can then inspire younger women around them to achieve what they want – to support others in business and be valued for it. I'm also aware that our industry structure leaves a lot of VAs potentially feeling isolated, so on the way to my end goal I work hard to help them feel connected to others.

This focus helps me decide what to do in my business each day. An opportunity that arises is checked against my big why, and if it aligns, I go ahead, but if it doesn't align, I let it go. This keeps me motivated, inspired and on track.

You may find that your big why is the sort of driver that appears across many areas of your life, not just business. If you could leave the world having impacted it in one way, what would it be?

What will keep you inspired?

What is your bigger picture?

As touched on above, you may have a more immediate driver that inspires you – your family for example. Or perhaps it's cash flow or going on a dream holiday. Whatever inspires you right now is also important to get clear on. You want to have smaller, bite-sized and measurable goals that you can celebrate on your journey. And please remember to celebrate those smaller wins! Acknowledge yourself for each step forward.

The family element is one you need to check on regularly – what does 'being there for my kids' mean to you?

Is it attending school events? Is it being there for pickup each day? Is it being present for your child in their first years? Whatever it is, check on it regularly and make sure your business is helping you achieve it. When we don't assess our 'reasons why', we can find that our business is doing the opposite: it's consuming us so much that we don't clock off when the kids are home, or we don't enjoy life because we are too tired from trying to fit it all in. Make sure your business is working for you rather than against you.

Remember that being a business owner means you work out what your priorities are, and you take the steps you need to take to make them come true. Anything is possible!

Do you have what it takes?

Being a business owner is worlds away from being an employee. And it's probably not at all like you'd expect. It takes incredible dedication, vision and self-discipline. Knowing your 'big why' will help you with this! You will have many moments where you'll want to throw it all in when it just gets too tough. But understanding exactly what you want to achieve from it all will help bring you back on track on even the hardest days.

Are you driven enough to work without being accountable to someone else? Yes, you'll have clients who you're accountable to, but what about all of the business administration and training for your business – the unbillable stuff? Will you be self-disciplined enough to stay on top of it?

Are you good at managing your time? If you're juggling family with your business, you probably won't have much time to focus on your business – not as much as you'd like, anyway. You'll need to manage your own life and then fit in your client jobs, your administration, networking, promotion etc. The best way to manage some of that time is to practice what you preach. As a VA, you tell other businesses to outsource the stuff they shouldn't or can't do, so you should be doing the same. Get help for those things that would otherwise slow you down or hold you back.

You'll also have things that come up that throw your time-management out of the window – you or a family member falling sick for example. How will you manage that? How will you ensure that your clients are not let down?

You'll also need to decide if you can manage conflict and negative feedback. Because you'll get it. Guaranteed. You'll have jobs that don't go well, you'll have people who you clash with, and you'll have trolls who want to keep you down. How will you manage that? Do you have great support around you, tough skin and the insight to grow from mistakes?

As you'll be working mainly online, do you have the communication skills required to run an effective service business? Customer service and communication is everything in a service-based business, and this is an area you need to be strong in.

If you've been used to regular income, think about if you can (or 'are able to') survive on an irregular income (or possibly no income for a while)? Cashflow can be a real bugbear when you are self-employed, especially for the first few years. Having some kind of backup plan for income is a really good idea. Starting up a business is a financial risk, and you need to consider all of your options. Speaking to your accountant or a financial planner about your financial needs and goals is a great first move.

Are you a people person? Can you build your community? Do you have the skills and determination to get out and network to build your community, stay in touch, give as you receive and build those relationships? You'll need a strong community to help both yourself and your clients as your business grows.

Doing some training, watching webinars or listening to podcasts where you can learn some great tips around the above areas is a great investment of your time. There are some great time-management strategies and skills you can learn to better cope with the challenges of running a business. It's also great to know you aren't alone on those days where you feel like absolutely everything is going wrong.

My current favourite podcasts are Renee Hasseldine's 'Leveraged & Loving It' and Sonya Statmann's 'Women in the Business Arena'. And make sure you check out the 'Outsourcing Mysteries Exposed' podcast by yours truly!

I also love checking out Skillshare.com for some short but useful training videos (you can find my training video there too for VA startups) which can explore anything from video editing, social media skills, communication skills, through to website development. Youtube also is a good resource (understatement there) for learning anything in business. Sometimes I'll allocate time to simply sitting down and taking in some of these things rather than doing the doing. They help with generating ideas and moving forward on areas you are stuck in.

Your personality type is important to understand when you work for yourself. Knowing what makes you tick, what stops you in your tracks and how best you communicate are all valuable. Understanding how other people tick is important too. Having a 'one-size-fits-all' approach to working with people in business is not going to work because we are all different. It's worth googling 'personality types' to learn about the key personality types and how they best function. It will help you understand yourself, your team and your clients which will help you better support them.

My favourite personality type tool is the Gary Smalley Personality Test. This simple test allocates you to one of the following categories – Lion, Otter, Golden Retriever or Beaver.

https://www.personality-and-aptitude-career-tests.com/
gary-smalley-personality-test.html

By answering a few questions you'll be able to identify your featured traits – you can fall into more than one. In fact, we all have elements of all categories. But the best thing about understanding the four categories is that you can use them to work more effectively with other people by identifying the traits they are displaying.

How you'd communicate with a Lion is different from how you'd communicate with a Golden Retriever. Their decision-making processes are different, and their strengths and weaknesses are different. These personality types can also form parts of your ideal client or your most suitable people to collaborate with.

What types of personalities does Gary Smalley's personality test reveal?

There are four types of personalities which are revealed through Gary Smalley tests.

They include:

1. The Choleric Lion

Lions are the leaders. You can get to know the powerful choleric through the way they walk in and take charge of everything. They usually are the bosses at work or somewhat considers them to be. Lions are decisive and are great problem solvers. If you are a lion in the Gary Smalley test, then you are an extrovert and believe in setting goals and achieving them fairly. Moreover, your personality has other traits like being a multi-tasker, hard-working and self-sufficient. Your personality as a lion is individualistic and is in continuous search of new opportunities and adventures.

On the flip side, your personality as a lion is very demanding and impatient along with being an impulsive and poor listener. You are quick tempered and irritable and are constantly making efforts to make your personality productive and purposeful.

2. The Sanguine Otter

If your Gary Smalley personality test reveals you to have traits like Otter then you are fun-seeking, excitable, cheerleader type who is fond of talking a lot. You will become a great motivator for others and will suffer in an environment where you are restricted to talk. Otters are extroverts and love to be at the centre of attention.

There is a lot of enthusiasm and energy but, you can also get distracted quite easily and quickly. An Otter's personality traits can make them irresponsible and selfish; however, your friendly nature can easily help others to forget your weaker tendencies.

3. The Loyal Golden Retriever

In the Gary Smalley personality test, one word that can explain Golden Retrievers is 'Loyal'. If you are a Golden Retriever, your level of loyalty is so intense that you will take an enormous amount of punishment or pain when in a relationship and will remain committed to it. You are willing to stay out of trouble and are an introvert who wants peace. Your dry humour will keep your companions happy and laughing all the time.

You avoid getting too involved in matters and prefer to sit back and watch; however, when you're aroused, you serve to be an efficient and competent person. Gary Smalley has rendered such a personality to the Golden Retriever who is sensitive, loves everyone and can blend in any situation.

4. The Melancholy Beaver

Another type of personality that is revealed in the Gary Smalley personality test is the Beaver. Gary has associated the word perfect melancholy with this type of personality traits because such people want to do everything properly and in order. If you're a Beaver, then you're an extreme introvert who details over labour. Your personality will shine in environments where standards, rules, and consistency are very important.

The perfectionist nature of a Beaver often makes such people prone to legalism and procrastination. Moreover, when there are unrealistic standards, they can also lack in expressing warmth within a relationship.

When it comes to being a VA, you don't have to be any specific one of these traits. It's more important to simply understand how you best work and how to work with those around you. Knowing your strengths and weaknesses and building a team around you to fill any gaps is a powerful tool in itself.

Myth buster: Anyone can be a VA!

I participate in a lot of Facebook groups that focus on mums in business. The Virtual Assistant industry is one that is predominantly full of women who want to work from home – a lot of those around children. Naturally, the concept of working as a VA comes up a lot in these groups. Want a new work from home business? Then be a VA! But is working from home as a Virtual Assistant right for you?

Providing support to business owners is serious stuff. Helping someone grow their business through administration, social media, writing, websites, reception, research, design and bookkeeping, (just to name a few), are not the sort of things you'd want to do at a low standard and expect money in return.

All around the world, thanks to increasing access to the Internet, it seems every person with access to a computer, thinks, 'Hey, this is the answer for me'. Maybe it is. Maybe it isn't.

The VA industry is incredibly broad. The services offered within it are so varied it's almost insane. And the quality of service across the industry is also extremely varied. Some people treat it as a hobby; some treat it as a job and some as a business. Some are amazing at it, and some truly suck.

If you come to me and ask how to become a Virtual Assistant, this is the advice I will give to you.

- If you don't have great communication skills – don't bother
- If you can't put your heart into the success of someone else's business – don't bother
- If you aren't willing to keep learning and training all the time – don't bother
- If you aren't willing to network and do the hard yards – don't bother
- If you can't respect and maintain confidentiality – don't bother

When you start your business, you'll have to invest some time, energy and money into it. And if you don't want to make the above points a priority, then you're wasting that time, energy and money. And for me? I don't want to see you fail, but more than that I don't want you diluting the quality of an incredible industry.

If you want to become a VA, a self-employed VA, here are my key tips for you.

- Make sure your communication skills are excellent
- Make sure you know why you want to do this and what success will look like for you
- Put money, time and effort aside to keep learning and growing
- Network, network, network – online AND offline
- Work with people who know the industry and know how to make it work
- Master the skills and services you want to offer
- Take great pride in yourself and your clients' successes
- Learn from your mistakes and own them

And above all, embrace the journey.

Confidence

Everyone ELSE has it together

Nearly every person I speak to reveals they lack confidence and feel like they're well behind everyone else. To them, everyone else is succeeding and living the dream. Everyone wants to present themselves to the world as a strong and competent business. But most likely, they're like a duck frantically treading water – looking calm on the top and working crazily underneath. Some business owners will be working on, or even stressing about the same things as you, while others have different issues that you'd never even considered.

Think about the many reasons why people start up their own business. There is a massive element of wanting to take control back of their lives but what inspired this need? For some, it's because they are battling a chronic illness which makes employment hugely stressful and unreliable. For others, it's raising a child with special needs, knowing that every day can be completely unpredictable. And for others again it's that desperate desire to feel accomplished and to achieve something. Or maybe it's the desire to get out of that financial rut that has plagued them for so long. Everyone has different reasons for deciding that self-employment is the best option for them, and in my experience, it's often adversity that has led them to this decision.

With these drivers in mind, you can imagine that running a business may be a good idea because you'd have more control, but the juggling act and the desire to be one person in your business and another person outside of your business can be incredibly exhausting. And when you're exhausted, you're often less likely to be able to ignore that inner voice of doubt, telling you that you're a fraud, that you're failing everyone, and that you should just give up.

Women seem to doubt their abilities more easily than they embrace and celebrate what they're doing well. They see what they're doing wrong, and not the many things they're doing right. But for most, once they get out there and start networking for their business, they put that to the side, and they focus on their business and what their business can do. And they don't reveal to you what's happening in their head or behind the scenes. In reality, you're comparing yourself to their 'showreel'. You assume that everyone else has it together. And because you do the same thing – i.e. put on your best face – everyone else thinks the same of you. Because that's how it's done. You don't put on your worst face when you go out networking – that simply won't work. But you do need to remember that we're all in the same business ocean, in our little boats, bumping along, doing our best . Most of us have holes in our boats, and when others aren't looking, we are bucketing out that water as best we can. Because that's life.

Everyone else does NOT have it all together. I've never met a person who has it all together. We all have our demons, so don't compare yourself to them. Just run your race and do your best. Have confidence that you are just like them - in your boat doing the best you can.

To grow your business, there's usually some element of discomfort and unknown. There will always be something happening in the background that isn't being revealed to the rest of the world.

Don't worry about falling 'behind' or being the 'newbie'. Starting your business venture and trying your best is a huge accomplishment that you should be very proud of. It's not easy – and the reality of becoming a business owner is not something we can learn at school – it's all on the job learning!

There is some truth to the old saying 'fake it till you make it' – show that you are a confident and strong person who is brave enough to step up and work for yourself. There will be things you need to learn, and barriers to overcome – but we've all been there. It's just part of the journey. You can also convince your subconscious to 'fake it till you make it' – if you tell yourself that you are confident, strong and brave, your subconscious will believe it. That's just how it works. And the more you believe and put those vibes out there, the more opportunities you'll see and take on.

Similarly, if you tell yourself you can't – your subconscious will believe that too. Empower yourself by speaking to yourself positively and proactively.

Finding a good mentor– someone you respect and admire – can be helpful here. They should be able to reassure you that they too have been where you are, and they are proof that you can get through it, with some hard work and determination. And a huge dose of faith.

The services you deliver in your business may not be unique, but because you're YOU, the way it's done and delivered will most likely be unique. Have faith that there are ideal clients out there for you, who you can tailor your service and delivery to, and who will give you more confidence to grow and stretch in your business. You might not know who they are yet, but if you don't, that should be a goal for your business – to discover who loves and needs what you can deliver - and life will become much easier!

Even the most accomplished business owner has something they're unsure about – but do they show it? No. That's what business is about – giving clients the confidence that we can deliver what they need and delivering on that promise. The challenges in the background are just part of the package.

When you were employed by someone else, did your boss' customers know about the back of house politics, the computer issues, the confusion about the new branding direction, budget or funding issues? Not likely. Now YOU are the boss. That's the only difference.

If it makes you feel any better, I already think you're pretty awesome because you've purchased this book and dedicated some time to learn from it. Well done!

Something else to consider is that the business challenges you're facing are great for your business research. Knowing how crazy it can all be behind the scenes, how insecure you can feel at times, the difficulty with asking others for help is great because:

1. You don't want others to see the reality of your business 'behind the scenes' and
2. It's really hard to let go and trust that someone will do it right

All of this is useful. If you can understand and relate to this, you might have a chance of understanding how most of your clients are feeling at least some of the time.

Anything that makes you feel insecure, worried or unsure about in your business is most likely something that other business owners feel too. You're in the business of supporting clients with this, so as you work through it yourself make sure you remember how it feels and what would be useful to you if a VA came along and offered to help you.

Can I handle success?

Some business owners are in a position that they're happy with – they don't want more growth. They're achieving their financial and time-based goals, and they're happy. In this case, they still need to be maintaining their business, keeping their toes in the market, but they may not wish to have a bigger business. If they're working the hours they want and achieving their income goals, then this is excellent.

Others are happy working the way they're working, but they are NOT achieving their financial goals. Or on the opposite side of the scale, they're working too many hours at the sacrifice of their family or desired lifestyle but potentially making the money they want. In this case, they need to be working smarter, not harder. They need to look at how they can grow without negatively impacting their family time.

I feel that this is often the hardest position to be in when faced with a potentially rewarding challenge. The itty bitty shitty committee says, "If you succeed, you'll have a bigger business, and you'll have to work more. You like the number of hours you're working, and you don't want to risk that." Or, "You already work too much, if you get bigger, you'll lose control of everything." Or even, "If you grow, more people will see you, and they'll realise you're just a big old fraud".

In this situation, it's important for your goals to factor in what the ideal result is for you. You may not want a global company or a team under you. But you may want more money or fewer hours working (or both!). The goals you pick need to resonate with this so that you can invest your heart into it.

And then there are others who are picturing a business that is much bigger, has staff or contractors helping them, and maybe even working from an office out of the home.

These people will need to try new things and take on additional people. This can be scary, but if a big business is what you want, you can do it!

When faced with the opportunity to grow the business further, reach more clients, make more money, grow your brand – some of us shy away because of the 'itty bitty shitty committee' on our shoulder telling us that we can't handle that success, that we'll only fail, or that our life will change and that's not comfortable.

This is your call. But if you don't 'feel the fear and do it anyway[1] you might lose out on some amazing opportunities and the potential for business growth. No one becomes a huge success without facing those fears and taking them on. There is fear around growth and growth around fear.

Whatever your situation, you need to consider whether the desired outcome is achievable and how you would work with it to make it work for you.

Can I invest more time or money into this unknown?

This is a question that we regularly ask ourselves. And it's worth noting that your clients are thinking of this too – especially before they hire you to help them.

Odds are, you will need to invest money into ventures before you can see the financial rewards. This can feel scary. When you're speaking to potential clients about the benefits you bring to their business regarding their time, their growth, and their money rewards – always think about these same factors and nut them out for your growth and ventures.

Speaking to an accountant is always a great place to start. They can help you with forecasting and strategies to meet your goals.

If your investment is going towards training, work out how that extra education will benefit you financially in the future.

---

1   © Susan Jeffers http://www.susanjeffers.com

How will it work for you? Consider the pros and cons before making investment decisions.

> "Worrying about coping with success has impacted my business and life in general. Self-belief and confidence is something that I have come a long way with and continue to work on, but there is always that annoying little voice in the back of my head telling me I'm not going to succeed, that I'm not good enough or smart enough to run a successful business! If it wasn't for that lack of confidence, I think I would have started my business earlier – it was only because fate stepped in and I was made redundant that I took the leap of faith!
>
> The single biggest factor in my managing of this worrying has without a doubt been the support I have found from other people, but especially from other VAs such as through virtuallyyours.com.au. To have that unwavering belief and support from so many other people, as well as the willingness to help as much as possible has helped me to grow as a person, VA and a businesswoman. While we may all be working as individuals, having that feeling of being part of a wider team and having that support, or even just a sounding board is an amazing thing!"

Kristy Fawdry
SORTED. Virtual Business Solutions

The business stories we often hear about, on repeat, are those massive "success stories" where someone came from nothing, and through using a specific simple strategy or process, they're now living the life of their dreams, earning six or seven figures – and you can too if you buy their program.

Most of these are just people making money selling you a dream. Be wary and always do your homework. Embrace your unique journey. Don't let your fear of failure drive you to seek a magic pill solution.

My pet hate on social media are those stories that are created to make you feel like you aren't good enough. And that you could be awesome if you just bought this one program. The people selling these ideas would say they're giving people hope and opportunity, but the reality is that they're preying on your vulnerability to sell a magic pill that doesn't exist. Yes, you can succeed, but those magic pills aren't the way. I've heard story after story of these people selling a solution that just didn't work out. They blame you for not doing everything they told you to do, but often, some of those 'steps to success' just don't resonate with you because they don't align with your beliefs. And that's why each journey is unique – what you will or will not do for success and what you define as success are unique to you.

How often have you heard big business names like Richard Branson talking about how tough it all was at the start, but they fought their way through the battle, and now they are 'on top of the world'! No one who is hugely successful has achieved it without taking some risks, whether they're financial or emotional. If it were easy – EVERYONE WOULD DO IT! It's getting through the rejections, the mistakes, the disasters that make you stronger.

A great startup story is that of Daniel Flynn from 'thankyou'. The startup for this now hugely successful venture was rocky. It's an amazing tale – check it out at https://au.thankyou.co/. When you hear Daniel's story, you'll find yourself asking – would I have kept going? Could I have done that? What would I have done in that situation?

The key to all these success stories is simply passion. Without a passion for what you're trying to achieve, picking yourself up again after a tough day, week, month or year, will feel impossible. But if you have a dream – you can get back up.

"Find your why. Why do you do what you do? Why are you going to go down that career path or launch that business? From my experience the why needs to go pretty deep because when the going gets tough it's the only thing that will keep you there."

Daniel Flynn, thankyou.com

Let's look at some of the excuses in business we use which stop us from succeeding.

I asked Virtual Assistants, 'What excuses do you tell yourself to ensure you don't succeed too much?' and these are some of the responses:

- If I succeed, I won't have time for my family anymore
- If I succeed people will think I'm full of myself
- If I get busier, I'll start letting clients down
- If I try, I won't know what I'm doing, and I'll fail
- I'm a mum, and I can't do all those networking things like I'm meant to, so I'll just put everything on hold until she finishes school
- Imposter Syndrome – even with all that I know, I don't ever feel I know enough

As you can see, there are so many perceived pressures around success and what it looks like. Knowing what success looks like to you is important.

I asked some of them, "For you, wouldn't success look like 'supporting fewer clients for more money? What would you say to yourself about achieving that?". And the general response looked like this: "Where are those clients that want to pay what we're worth? I know my worth but finding a client that does too, well that is the hard bit."

The problem shifted when the definition of success shifted. Instead of worrying about letting everyone down, or being an imposter, you can focus on finding the sort of client who values what you offer and will pay the right amount. Finding the sort of success that suits the lifestyle you want, the hours you want to work and the pressure you can take on.

- Who needs the solution you have to offer?
- Who is the best fit for you?
- Who are you least likely to let down, because you're a good match?
- Who values what skills and knowledge you have?

Focus on finding the right client, and you'll be less likely to 'fail'. Focus on the positives and always see the good and the bad days as lessons for growth. Focus on these, and you'll find a success that doesn't terrify you.

But, what if I fail?

These four little words are the biggest block and the loudest voice in our heads – "What if I fail?"

Well, what if you do? What would happen? Would worlds collide? Would you die of shame? Literally? Unlikely.

"You can have results or excuses, but you can't have both."

Arnold Schwarzenegger

Did you know that the most experienced, successful business owners have one thing in common? They've all failed. Again, and again. But, they've taken that opportunity to learn. Failure is only a true failure if you fail to learn.

The best products, the best recipes, the best medicines, have all come about after many failures. Trying something new, branching out, giving it a go – are all risks. But you WILL need to take some risks if you want to succeed in business. If you can't handle taking some risks and some, if not most of them, not working then maybe business is not for you. Staying in your comfort zone is a sure way to stagnate and get left behind.

My motto is 'feel the fear and do it anyway' inspired by the book of the same name, by Susan Jeffers. It's the motto I used to start my business, and still inspires me today. Don't get me wrong, you still need to assess risk to make smart choices. But I've learned that almost every step forward carries an element of risk.

If you're not feeling at least slightly awkward in what you're doing, maybe you're not doing enough.

There are so many 'lines' and 'mottos' about failure, stepping up, failing to fail and all of that. And they all sound great and very inspiring. But the reality can be hard-hitting. That horrible heavy feeling in your belly and that overwhelming feeling of shame. It's human. We've all been there, and we will be again. The best we can do is to work on how we are going to respond to failure, what we will learn from it and what we can do to minimise failure based on what we've learnt.

I encourage you to consider what failing looks like to

you. Your goals may change and evolve, but any progress, be it advancing the business or learning something new, is all positive. So, what exactly is failing?

For some, it's letting clients down. This can be through offering more than you can deliver, failing to communicate effectively or dropping the ball. For other's it's not being able to grow your business and going back to employment, believing you need to tell people that you've failed at something. Many business owners speak of 'Imposter Syndrome' – where they fear they'll be found out for not knowing as much as they 'should' and for 'pretending' to be better than they are. Or perhaps it's starting a project and not being able to complete it, or it not being received well by the intended audience. And of course, for many of us, it's a combination of all the above.

Which of the above describes your vision of failure? Or is it something different again? What is the likeliness of the failure occurring? What are you doing to avoid it? If it does happen – what will you do?

Some of your responses may form part of your business contingency plans, such as if you let a client down or a project fails. Other areas, such as your fear of being 'found out for the fraud you are' can be addressed by discussing your concerns with a mentor or undertaking any training to fill gaps you've identified. Do what you can to address your concerns but don't spend overly long worrying about what you can't control. Have faith in the skills and services that you can offer and stay true to yourself.

Running your own service-based business is so personal – every fear feels close to your heart.

Being in business, you probably have someone who you admire and look up to. Someone who is doing what you hope to do one day – living the dream. It may be worth asking them what their fears are (if you can). Ask what failure would look like to them. You'll probably find that they aren't so far from your own. Our fear of failure can be the biggest hurdle we face in business.

Failure can be in all sorts of forms. It can be something as simple as forgetting to call someone back, letting a client down on a task and dropping the ball. It can be failing to communicate with subbies correctly. It could also be in the form of an idea you want to bring to market, a new focus for your business. We all try not to fail at something we do, but we need to be realistic - it's going to happen at some point. For me, failure is an education process. I look at it, analyse it, own it and learn from it. I'm not afraid of failure because if I do happen to fail at it, the outcome is I'll grow from it. Don't get me wrong failure sucks sometimes but it doesn't have to be negative.

Kirstie Stark
JMK Business Solutions

👉 Case study #1: A day in the life of a VA dealing with her inner chatterbox (also known as the voice of self-sabotage)

New business – Birgit Livesey

Dealing with self-sabotage is something that happens to me regularly. I call it 'my Inner Chatterbox'. Why? Because it never shuts up, hardly ever is positive and supportive and without constant 'care' could take over my day, week, hell, even my life!

So, what is it saying?

Here are a few examples:

- "If you do this, what will others say?"
- "This is way beyond your skill set, you can NEVER do this/achieve this."
- "What if I go ahead with this decision and I fail?"
- "I'd rather not do this because it is more than I can handle."
- "You will never work with this type of client. You are dreaming!"
- "What will others say (about you and your business)?"

How do I deal with this little, uninvited and annoying voice? I have learnt ways to silence it. For me, reading one book on how to face these fears (Feel the Fear and Do It Anyway!" by Susan Jeffers) has completely changed the way

I approach certain aspects in my life and business. It is a constant process of evaluating and taking action. But it's worth it because I am worth it and it will lead me to live the life that I truly want and deserve.

How am I unique?

You, my dear, are YOU. And no one does YOU quite like you do! Or in the words of Dr Seuss, 'Today you are YOU, that is truer than true, and there is no one alive, who is youer than you'.

There are lots of components to a business that you'll need to set up and deliver. How you do that will be unique to you. I highly recommend that you don't model yourself so closely on someone that you become a replica of them – it won't ring true for you or your clients. Use your own words and always believe in what you're delivering. Don't stress about what other VAs are doing – odds are, your ideal client is different to theirs as is your service delivery . If it's the same (rare!) consider if there is a big enough market for that and if not, what you can tweak to tap into a better piece of the market while still staying true to you.

Let's look at some of the different components of a business and consider how YOU have approached each.

Business structure

Are you set up as a sole trader? A company? Under a trust? Hopefully, you spoke to your accountant first to ensure you have the best structure for you. One that benefits you and supports you in the growth of your business.

Location

Are you working from home or outside of the home? If at home, do you have a dedicated room? A dedicated desk? A cool little office in the yard?

Hours

What hours are you working on your business? The 9-5 grind? Evenings? School hours? Weekends?

Services

What are the services you're offering? Phone support? Diary Support? Web development? Copywriting? Marketing? Social Media? Honestly, this list could go on, but the services you have selected will be the ones that resonate with you.

Target market

Who are you aiming your service at? Who would most benefit from your services? How are you targeting them?

Please remember that target markets need to be specific – simply saying that you are targeting home-based business owners, or sole traders, for example, is not targeted marketing. You need to drill down and be specific about your ideal client, so you can create, promote and deliver your product to meet a need best.

Terms of payment

What are your terms? Upfront payments? Monthly retainers? 7-day terms? Deposit up front? At the very least, make sure that you're not doing work for free. Never continue to provide a service to someone who has an outstanding account.

Delivery process

How do you deliver your product? How do you format your proposals? How do you follow up? How do you communicate with your clients? How do you measure your results and what do they look like?

Marketing

Where are you marketing and in what format? Are you networking? (I hope that's a yes!). Are you using paid or sponsored advertising? Are you using referral rewards? Do you request and encourage testimonials? Do you use sales funnels? What does your client journey look like?

Quality control

How do you assess the ongoing quality of your service delivery? Do you ask for feedback? How do you use and respond to that feedback?

Referrals

Do you have a way of tracking, acknowledging, and rewarding others for referring work to you?

Pricing

How have you priced your service? Have you calculated what you need to be charging to meet your financial objectives? Is it a fair price for the market? Is your target market tailored to be able to afford your rate?

There are so many factors that make up a business. And when you put them all together, you create your own unique business. Add that special ingredient, you, and you have something wonderful!

Don't feel that you must be bigger than you are – stay true to your moral and ethical standards and don't worry about comparing yourself to everyone else.

Myth buster: I'm too introverted to run a business!

BUSTED!

Guess what? We have a fascinating and important Industry on our hands. Entrepreneurs who naturally shine behind the scenes!

As we all know, most entrepreneurs are outgoing,

confident, ideas people. They have a million ideas and the confidence to put it out there and tell everyone how great they are. However, their success can often rely on them tapping into the skills of those who can slow down, see the detail, action the bits and pieces and deliver it without fanfare. Forces combined, the entrepreneur and their amazing behind the scenes person can achieve and deliver wonderful things.

So, what happens when that behind the scenes person needs to step up and tap into their entrepreneurial superstar? What happens when instead of just being behind the scenes, they need to network, inspire and convince others to sign on the dotted line?

This can be incredibly intimidating and tough. But it must be done if you want to be a self-employed individual. However, if you own it and you take pride in yourself and how you work, you'll find that these things holding you back are what can inspire your prospects to hire you.

What do I mean by that? Well, put yourself in the shoes of the entrepreneur – your prospect - the person you want to work with. Consider what is missing for them? Odds are, it's someone who knows how to deliver their service well but from behind the scenes. They may feel scared of letting someone into their secret business bits for fear of judgement or of someone stealing their ideas. If they met you, and you were a genuine, dedicated, hardworking specialist in your field – do you think that that would inspire confidence in them? I think it would.

I have a couple of VAs who support me in different areas, but my main VA is an incredible woman whose skills allow me to shine. She knows how the reign me back in when I get too excited about a new shiny object, and she's great at the tasks that I am not good at. When you run your own business, the last thing you want to worry about is your assistant trying to be front and centre of your brand. You don't want them running off and creating a business just like yours. You don't want them to become your competition. You want them to support you, understand your business thoroughly, have ideas and passion, but have only one business they want to be the face of – their own.

Some VAs are quite extroverted – but they love helping your business shine because that's what drives them. I'm not saying you shouldn't hire an extrovert. What I'm saying is that if you're an introverted VA, you also have a lot to offer.

The family juggle

As I write this (the first draft anyway!) my little one (Ruby, aged four) is in a gymnastics class, and I'm beyond tired with my sore 27-week pregnant belly hogging leg space that the laptop wants. It's Friday, and Friday is one of my 'Ruby days' – one of my days where I don't work (except when she's in this class), and I'm simply 'Mum'. Of course, being mum means more than just playing with my kid. It means getting a million things done around the house, running errands, working out what we are going to be eating for the next day or so (I rarely manage to plan beyond that) and, well frankly, all the jobs that aren't associated with my business. No rest for the wicked!

I'm embarrassed to admit that that first draft was written three years ago now! My setup has changed yet again. I now have eight year old Ruby and three year old Ella.

When I started Virtually Yours, I was working part-time. Then, a year or so in, I went full time into Virtually Yours. A few years later I got married and added a baby to the equation. Now I've got two. What works for me, may not work for you, but I've found a fairly good balance by having a couple of days a week where someone else has Ella, and luckily for me, my hubby is self-employed too, so he gets that gig around his work commitments. So effectively I've gone from originally working seven days, to working three days per week when I had 1 child and now down to two days with two kids. To be honest, the less time I'm given, the faster I get stuff done. That's not to say I'm not excited about what I could now achieve once both kids are in school!

Some people can get done what they need to get done in this time; some can't. Some can't utilise partners, parents/in-laws or family/daycare due to various circumstances. Some are lucky enough to rely on support from a family member for a day or so during the week – it's about finding a balance that works for you and allows you to meet your objectives. Remember that your objectives are not only work based – they're based on time spent with family, time spent nurturing yourself. Those days are just as important. For me, my current situation is ideal. I'm with my daughter five days of the week, and then two days, between school hours, are heads down bums up. That works for me right now.

I'd like to share a few case studies from VAs who are in various situations and how they are currently managing the juggle.

👉 Case study #2: The truth about running a home-based business while raising teenagers

Monique Eddy, A Virtual Copywriting Monstar: Two teenagers, one out of home.

It's not that hard!

Many VAs decide to start up their home-based business after having children so they can be home with their family and not return to the often inflexible 'corporate rat race'. They're smart. I honestly didn't think of that...

I started my business once my kids were at school and I had some 'spare hours' to concentrate on building my business.

This year marks my 9th year in business, and I have two wonderful teenage kids (one who's moved out for Uni) and a thriving business.

Perhaps I've been blessed with two very well behaved, down to earth, sensible teens, but I've found running my VA/Copywriting business while raising two teens quite easy. Even when the school holidays hit.

Here's how running a home business and raising teenagers is made easy:

- They're at school from 8am to 4pm, giving me an uninterrupted 8-hour work day

- They don't need 'mum helpers' for excursions or in-class help, so I'm never called away to help the school (gosh, how embarrassing would it be for mum to be at high school!)
- If I'm ever stuck with technology, I ask my teenagers, and they ALWAYS have the answer (and often joke that I should pay them for their knowledge!)
- They sleep until at least midday on school holidays, so I work all morning, take the afternoon off to run them all over town, and then continue working after hours
- They're self-sufficient, no longer needing me to help with bathroom duties or homework (in fact, their homework often goes over my head)
- They can help with the cooking, so if I'm swamped with work I know we'll all be fed
- They can make their school lunches, get themselves up in the morning, make breakfast, get dressed and get everything together for their day so I'm not running around frantic all morning and can start my day feeling fresh
- If I ever want to go to a business event, they're capable of looking after themselves, and I don't need to arrange sitters for them

My life while running a business and raising teenagers is streamlined.

I've recently had the older one move to go to Uni, but the routine with the other teen continues (and in ways, she's more full on with 2 jobs, basketball and friend commitments). I do work a little harder now (I charge what I'm worth and don't fold as much) as I need to pay for Uni accommodation and maintain two households which is a tad stressful (Centrelink doesn't help working parents with kids who want to study for a secure future!).

What I miss the most is dinner time. This has always been our together time, where the kids and I would sit down at the table and eat together, sharing our day and listening to each other. I raised my kids with the 'no secrets' rule, so we're pretty close. Now Tori and I sit alone and have lovely chick chats!

I think my communication skills have been enhanced from working virtually. You need to be able to communicate clearly with your clients, and I've applied this in my personal life with my teenagers too. As with my clients, if my teenagers have a problem, they know they can approach me, and we'll find a solution together.

I take my hat off to those with young children.

Juggling work/life with teenagers is easy! I think all credit should go to home-based business owners who have young children at home who demand so much more attention. Hang in there; it DOES get easier.

👉 Case study #3: The truth about running a business while raising young children

Kristie Stark, JMK Business Solutions: Two young children, one with medical needs.

It's been 10 years since I started my VA business and eight years now since I took the plunge and worked only for myself in my business. I love what I do and wouldn't change it as I don't think I could hold down a permanent full-time job. You see not only am I a Virtual Assistant with a successful business, I am also a mum to a special needs child.

Having a child with special needs certainly makes it harder, a lot harder in fact, but if you have to work like so many of us do, then being a VA is certainly the job I'd pick.

So much of our life is consumed by my daughter. There are good days, but many are extremely challenging. We have Dr's and specialist appointments, visits to the Children's Hospital, issues at school and challenges at home. I've adapted extremely well in being able to work "remotely" working on the iPad in waiting rooms at appointments. The key is being organised, extremely organised. On those days I plan my work so what needs to be completed can be done on the iPad. I might squeeze in an extra hour's work the night before to take the pressure off me that day. I do whatever I can to ensure my clients aren't impacted.

Being realistic and understanding the number of billable hours you can work is vital and I never ever over commit on our workload. To me letting down our clients is not an option. Learning to say no to a timeframe was hard but saying yes and not delivering was even harder to swallow.

There are days where I'm productive and get 6 hours of work completed, but then there are the days where I'm lucky to get 2 hours done. It's those days I give up and decide I need to be mum today and as soon as the kids are in bed, I head back into the office to restart my day. It's usually those nights the kids have me up a few times, and I'm lucky to get 4 hours sleep.

For me, my work and business are my escape where I forget about all the challenges we face and focus on helping my clients. Honestly, it's what keeps me sane. Don't get me wrong; there are days where it all gets too much, where I'm exhausted, and I question if I should give it all up, pour myself a bourbon, have a cry and let it all out. I know I'd be shattered if I had to walk away as I'm proud of the business I've created which is why now growing my team to be able to run the business on its own if I had to step aside for a while is important to me.

Being a successful VA and business owner is rewarding, and it takes commitment, drive and hard work. Doing it with a special needs child takes twice as much drive, commitment, flexibility and hard work but I'm proof you can be a VA with a successful business and look after a special needs child.

Case study #4: Running a business while raising teenagers with extra needs

Susie de Andrade, Adept VA: Three teenage kids, one with Autism/ADHD.

The Family Juggle – How do I do it?

Firstly, I try to be realistic!

I dream about how I'm going to grow my business, learn heaps of skills and have lots of subbies. But really, my family life is so overwhelming at the moment that I need to remember why I started this business in the first place – for flexibility. I've found that I don't have a lot of time for chargeable work. I know the amount of work I'm willing to do, and I've rarely gone over. If it happened continually, I'd have to outsource.

We're a family of five, including three teenagers and a dog. My youngest (13) has mild Autism Spectrum Disorder and ADHD. I spend a fair bit of time at appointments, researching, and attending ASD support and social groups. After school hours are dedicated to my daughter's activities and homework. There are still activities for my older children, driving lessons, sports, taxi service, etc. I also spend a fair amount of time cooking healthy food and baking. There's some voluntary work and a little bit of time with the hubby and our social life between all that!

So many activities mean I need to be organised.

No surprises there. Just as well my background is diary co-ordination, and I just love my Google Calendar! I wouldn't survive without it.

All time's accounted for – appointments, client work, kids' activities, exercise, cleaning and even what we're having for dinner. And, it's colour coded – red is for appointments, green is for my stuff, blue for the kids, different colours for different clients, pink for a few smaller clients, aqua for non-chargeable work, etc.

Where possible, I try to do work in blocks. I've allotted a certain amount of time for a client, and I try to do everything I can for that client before swapping over to another, so I don't lose time in transition.

I also like to get as much client work out of the way at the beginning of the week and keep the end of the week, particularly Fridays, for admin, VA learning and other projects. That way I have a buffer in case I have extra appointments or things go wrong. Also, rather than skip from project to project, one week I'll focus on admin, the next one on learning, another concentrate on research for my daughter, etc., again, so that I'm not losing too much time working out where I'm up to. At least that's the plan!

The truth is that the last 10 weeks have been a disaster!

I haven't managed any of my other projects, and apart from invoicing, all other admin has gone out the window!

I've collapsed at times in an exhausted heap, near tears and ready to give up.

I was after flexibility, but I also need to be flexible.

I'm constantly having to put off plans and just get through the week. Children can be so emotionally draining at times, but I can also see that things will improve, so I still have my goals and dreams, and I keep trying to chip away at them.

I never forget Martin Luther King Jr's quote:

"If you can't fly then run if you can't run then walk, if you can't walk then crawl, but whatever you do you have to keep moving forward."

So, the family juggle all comes down to four simple things... be realistic, be organised, be flexible and never give up!

Staying motivated

This is something that I can relate to as much as I love my business (and I can't stress that enough), I still go through days or hours or weeks or months where I am just not into it.

Sometimes the slump is a short one, an afternoon or morning where you're just not feeling it, and it's all hard work. Something like this could be alleviated by a simple walk outside in the fresh air or a change of location. I'll often pack up my laptop and walk down to my nearby café which means I've gotten some fresh air and then with a new location my headspace feels different. I do this so often that my café knows what I want to order, and they keep me topped up with soy hot chocolates.

For some, a walk with the dog, with your kid/s or alone can make a huge difference. And if you're worried about wasting time, you can always listen to a podcast while you're walking. I like the sounds of the world going around.

If you're lucky like me and you have a nice park or a spot in your house or backyard where you can sit and chill and have a coffee (or even better for your brain, a glass of water) then definitely make the most of it.

When you get back to your workspace create a list that you can tick off as you work. It's satisfying but also keeps you on track. Lists are particularly good for those days where you feel like you aren't getting anything done. Break the list down, and you'll realise you are moving forward, so don't stress!

If your slump is a little more 'long-term' and you're finding it all overwhelming, you can try a technology detox. One of my treats this year was going away with a couple of friends to the Seven Sisters Festival where we just chilled out, without our laptops, without playing on phones, all weekend. It was bliss. It can be so hard to detox these days when you're so used to using technology to get the answers you need (even from chats with friends – what was the name of that actor again?) but even more so when you're a virtual assistant. I bow down to those who can step away so easily from the tech.

A VA friend of mine, Kristen, told me that every Sunday her family has a phone free day where they turn off mobile roaming data. I love how this is a regular thing.

Another thing that works for me is to stop and clean up the office and put what you need to do up on the wall to keep you on track moving forward. I've got my massive whiteboard, and that has certain things on it that will keep me on track with mastermind or training or webinars etc. Way too often I find my office covered in toys and junk that the kids have brought in – it drives me crazy. So, I do a big clean to reclaim my space which in turn clears my head. There's nothing quite like a floor covered in Lego and lid-less markers to reduce your motivation.

Another thing you can do is have a mentoring session. If you're really, really struggling and you need a reboot and some new direction, then you can have a mentoring session, or you can catch up with a biz friend and have a coffee and a chat with them. That can be good. My business runs co-working days which are so good for this. Being able to catch up with a peer and sitting down working next to them can be hugely motivating.

The other thing I often do (because it works for me) is to rejig things and freshen things up in my business. Create something new because if you're doing the same thing all day every day, it gets boring. I mean you're human, so if you feel like, "I am sick of doing this", then think about how you could change it up and how you can make it a little bit more exciting and invigorating for you.

Training is another way to get motivated and away from the grind. Allocate some time regularly to listen to or attend some training in areas that benefit you and your business. It's never going to be a waste of time!

They're my main tips for getting your mojo back and getting motivated. Here they are again:

- Grab a coffee, cold water or iced tea, and sit in the backyard in the sun or in the shade or your balcony or wherever it might be. I find that if I go and sit on the couch that is a bad idea as I end up staying there! I need to go outside or something like that and have my coffee or cold drink
- Make a list. You can batch it; you can do it any way you like, you can add to it, so you look like a superstar by the end of the day as you have worked on all those great things
- Go for a walk
- Technology detox
- Clean your office

- Get some mentoring
- Chat with a biz friend
- Work from a café
- Change it up and create something new for your business
- Listen to some training stuff. Just stop doing the work stuff and listen to some training recordings.

YOUR OFFERING

***

Skills and services

The Virtual Assistant Industry is very broad however most people decide to become a VA and visualise themselves using their own key set of skills. What skills do you currently have that will help both you and your clients?

Often VAs come from a PA or EA background, or they're returning to work after raising a family. And sometimes VAs start off thinking they have nothing to offer but trust me; you have skills! You need to identify them.

I love having a mentoring session where we uncover all the great skills someone has, that they hadn't even considered previously. Being a mum, for example, requires time management, communication, serious patience and negotiation skills. And many mums volunteer their time coordinating school fundraisers or events or supporting local charity groups. They do these things using skills they take for granted but are valuable in the VA world.

Your skills

To uncover some of the skills you're bringing to the table I'd like you to consider what sort of skills are involved in the activities you currently do or have done in the past. Which skills come up most often – are they the sort of things you enjoy doing and find the easiest? Often the things we take for granted are skills that we naturally excel at. We assume because they're so easy to us that they aren't valuable. But everyone has a different natural skill set. Consider your partner, for example - are their skills the same as yours? Do the things they do naturally match up with yours? What about your family members and friends? You can probably identify other peoples' skills more easily than your own! Feel free to ask some friends or family for feedback on the sort of things they think you're great at (if you need to).

When you can identify your skills, you can start to think about what sort of services would be good for you to offer. You may even find that what you want to offer is a skill you're yet to develop. That's ok – start working on how, where and when you're going to grow those skills. Knowing what your skill gaps are is just as important as knowing what your skills are.

You will need to learn to keep your business alive and fresh constantly. The virtual industry is ever evolving, and new programs and program updates are constantly happening – never assume that the skills you have now are all you'll need. Keep an eye on gaps as they appear and make sure you allocate time and a budget to filling those gaps regularly.

You'll never know it all.
Every day there is something new to learn.
Don't drown in this thought – allocate time
weekly or monthly to learning new things.

When you know what sort of skills you have, think about how those can benefit your business and how they can be turned into a service. At the same time, think about who needs those services. Who are the people who wake up each day and think 'man, that (service) is such a pain for me – I wish there were an easier way to get it done.'

If the services you think you could be offering are targeted towards a specific type of client, this is great. It will make marketing easier and will help you streamline your services.

I've borrowed an article by Christie Mims from The Revolutionary Club because it's spot on and I believe it's a must-read. There are lots of great tips on that site so make sure you head over and check it out.

Three ways to uncover your talent and skills

Christie Mims, www.therevolutionaryclub.com

Have you ever sat there and thought:

"Ugh, I don't like what I'm doing at my job now—but what would I would be great at doing?"

"I'd love to make a career change, but how do I figure out what my real skills are?"

"There's got to be something that's a better match for me, but what?"

One of the most difficult parts of deciding which career path to pursue is figuring out what you're great at—other than what you're doing at your current (unfulfilling) job.

But don't worry: You are already more amazing than you give yourself credit for. In fact, you have plenty of job-related talents and skills—you just need to uncover them. To get started, ask yourself these three questions.

1. What do I love about my career?

Take out your most recent resume (yes, I know—ugh) and take a serious look at all of the jobs and responsibilities you have had. If you're just starting out, think about school, volunteer, and extracurricular activities, too.

Now, circle the things that you most liked doing. What,

specifically, were your favourite parts of each job?

Once you've done that, think about any job tasks that don't appear on your formal resume, but that you enjoyed—like mentoring new employees, leading employee orientation, choosing the flower arrangements for the office, or throwing happy hours, for example. Jot those down, too.

All of these activities and tasks that you enjoy are worth examining because they're likely tied to some of your greatest strengths. Throwing a happy hour could be related to a talent for organisation and event planning. Running employee orientation could mean you have a gift for training and communication or professional development.

Spend some time thinking about what you liked and why—and that's your first clue to where your career could go next.

2. Where do I lose track of time?

What hobbies, activities, or tasks occupy your full attention so much so that you are completely engaged in the present moment? You look up at the clock, thinking that no time has passed, and poof! Three hours have gone by.

These could be aspects of your current job (brainstorming names for the next product launch, working with the graphic design team on artwork for an upcoming ad), or they could be part of your personal life-being with children, blogging, or helping your friend craft a business plan, for example.

Start noticing these moments of time passing, and ask yourself: "What was it that I loved about that activity? What kept me so engaged?" Whatever it was is most likely tied to a talent or interest that could easily become a transferable work-related skill—or even your next career.

3. What are my greatest strengths?

Finally, take a moment for self-reflection and ask yourself: "What do I think are my greatest strengths?" Be proud—list things that you normally wouldn't say about yourself and brag a little bit.

And then, if you're feeling brave (and I hope that you are by now) email three people in your life who you trust and ask them what they find most inspiring about you. It can feel awkward to ask, but tell them that you're doing some career exploration and value their opinion and feedback. I guarantee you'll be surprised and intrigued by what you hear in response.

Now, take a look at all this information you've put together.

- What themes or trends do you notice?
- How does it feel to look at all of those lists, chock full of talents and skills?
- What have you learned about what you are good at?

Maybe you've found that your eye for detail, crazy clean

desk, and ability to always make people feel comfortable and motivated means that you're destined for success in company leadership. Or that your love of fashion, long articulate emails, and witty sense of humour merit exploring the blogging world.

Don't feel pressured to get the answer exactly right at this moment—instead, allow yourself to just explore possibilities. And take a deep breath of relief! You've now armed yourself with a map of your talents and skills, and you can start thinking about what to do with them next.

***

Services

If you have a few different skills but can't see a pattern emerging to develop services and people who need them, you can always ask friends, family or peers if they see a theme evolving. If they can't either, it may be worth booking in for a discovery session with a business specialist, like me! https://www.virtuallyyours.com.au/discovery-session/

You'll be told time and time again that niching will help you create a streamlined and more effective business. And this is 100% true. But don't worry too much if you have no idea what area to niche in straight away. Sometimes it takes trial and error, some research and evolution for the niche to happen.

A niche can be the service you offer, or the type of

people you offer it to, or both. Sometimes your services are general administration, but your niche may be around the industry and people within that industry that you provide the service too.

For example, you may have background knowledge of the Health Sector and could support practitioners and Allied Health professionals with their business administration.

You may understand the administration behind Research Consulting and could support Research Consulting businesses with their analysis processes.

Or you may, on the other hand, specialise in the service and offer that service to a variety of industries. For example, you may specialise in setting up and running the Infusionsoft CRM. It might not matter what sort of business you help, but the niche is the CRM.

For those of you who have been in business for some time and have no idea how you should be niching, don't fret. You probably already have a little bit. If not, take a good look at the services you're offering (how specific and unique are they?) and the people you are supporting (what do they have in common?).

When streamlining your service offerings ask yourself:

- Are you offering too many services? (do you look like you are 'ok' at a lot of things instead of amazing at a couple of things?)

- Who needs those services?
- Do the people who need these services align with your view of your ideal client?
- Do prospects know how they would use you for these services? (sometimes they can't see how it would all work, and so they shy away)

Guess what? People don't resonate with you if you have too many service options. You can't be awesome at everything, and you can't be passionate about everything. And people want awesome, and they want passionate. Because awesome, passionate people create awesome, passionate things. And that's what people will part with their money for. So be awesome and passionate! No pressure, of course.

Who wants your awesome services? Are there enough of these people for you to provide your service to? Will they pay you well for it? Are these people the sort of people you want to work with, who will keep you from losing inspiration, and who will keep you being awesome?

And do those people know what they need to do to get the ball rolling? Are you educating people about what they need to do so that you can deliver the services they need? Do they have a phone chat with you? Do they have a brainstorming session? Do they send you some documents? What do they need to do? Make it clear.

We will explore some of the process and delivery aspects later in this book.

Your target market

Your target market, much like your niche, can be hard to work out for some people. But unless you know who needs your services, it's going to be very hard to find clients. Your target market is simply the type of people you want to target your marketing to. The people you most want to help. The more specific you are about these people, the better your marketing will be. When working on your target market, think about the sort of person who can't live without the service you offer; the sort of person who loves the way you present yourself, how you deliver your services and who can afford and will invest in your help. You want the sort of person who thinks your service is awesome.

Understanding this person, or 'avatar' will help you develop your marketing and your product. You need to connect to your avatar in all your branding and communication and your service development.

Consider this person.

- What sort of work do they do?
- When do they work?
- How do they work?
- How old are they?

- What gender do they identify with?
- What is their family structure?
- What do their weekends look like?
- How do they support their clients?
- What inspires them?
- What barriers do they face?

When thinking about that avatar belonging to a set industry, you can ask questions about how they work. For example, a real estate agent. They may be female, aged 35-40, with two school aged kids, loves sporting activities for the whole family, works during school hours.

But you could also explore the real estate part:

- Are they private or commercial real estate?
- Are they part of a company or an independent agent?
- Do they manage rentals?
- Are they new and inexperienced, wanting to get a strong fresh foothold into the industry, or are they a well-known, reputable name?
- Do they currently manage their paperwork, tradies, phones, books and phones?
- Have they had an assistant before?
- Do they know how to work with a VA?

All these factors can help drive your marketing and guide your service offering.

And when you're clear about these things, you make it so much easier for the client to understand how you can support them.

You need to know as much as possible about your ideal client. Not only about what they love and hate, but also where they hang out for personal time and for work time. Knowing where to target your marketing will save you money. You may have to invest a little time and money into researching your target market, but it's worth it in the long run. When setting up your business structure, ensure that it includes ways that you can identify and measure where your leads are coming from and which ones are most likely to convert. The sooner you set these systems up in your business, the easier it will be to understand and connect with your target market.

Here are some questions you need to consider when identifying your target market:

1. What problem do I solve?
2. Who suffers from this problem?
3. Who suffers the most from this problem and has the most to lose if this problem isn't resolved? (Is there enough demand from these people?)
4. What is uniquely consistent about this group of people?
5. Do I know what the demographic, geographic, psychographic and behavioural traits of this group are?
6. How is my solution unique and irresistible for these people?

Based on the above information, you can start to create an Avatar - the person who is the ideal collection of the above data, the person who is most likely to buy from you. You should know as much as possible about your Avatar including where they live, their age, family structure, hobbies, behaviours, strengths, weaknesses etc.

When you have your Avatar (and you can modify those traits as you learn more about what works and what doesn't), you can target your solution and your marketing to them, with the aim of attracting these types of people into your business.

Myth buster: I don't just want you to save me time!

Many VAs are offering prospective clients the awesome benefit of "saving time" and "giving you your time back", and I don't think that's enough anymore.

Even though we are all rushed for time these days – more than ever before – the promise of saving me time or giving it back isn't enough to ease my business pains. Yes, I'd like more time. But I would rather swap my time from the tasks that make me groan, to the tasks that give me tingles! Not more time – just fewer LSTs! (Life Sapping Tasks).

Picturing you "giving me more time" is a bit exhausting...I

mean, what does that even mean? What do I want from you? I want results!

Here are examples of what I want to see in my business:

- I want those videos transcribed and loaded to my site
- I want my procedures written up and looking gorgeous, ready and waiting for when I have new staff, a holiday or, heaven forbid when I want to sell my business!
- I want someone to manage my LinkedIn account, so I'm not missing opportunities
- I want someone who can return those calls that involve explaining what it is we do and how we help others

I want real things, and I want you to tell me you can do them.

When you say you can save me time, you give me a job. That job is to now think of what I could pass on to you. Too hard! I don't have time...

What I need from you is specifics. Tell me you understand what my pain points are. Tell me you can make that pain go away.

A good plumber doesn't just say they can save you time. And in fact, that is something they do inevitably deliver – most services are there to save us time or effort. The plumber tells us how they will ease our pain. They'll fix your blocked drains. They'll repair that leak in the wall. They'll install your dishwasher and make you smile every time you go to wash the dishes.

Be SPECIFIC. Tell me which pain YOU ease. And if I'm your ideal client, I'll come knocking on your virtual door and beg you to come and help me out.

FOUNDATIONS

***

Insurance and legal questions

Do you need insurance?

Odds are, if you look at the litigious world we currently live in, you could benefit from insurance. Finding insurance that is right for your unique structure, however, can be very challenging. As can finding an insurance broker who understands your business. It's worthwhile having a face to face meeting with an insurance broker so that you can show them how you plan to work, and they can give you appropriate advice.

Everyone has a unique set up, and I am not an insurance advisor, so I can't advise you on what you need. However, I would go so far as to say that you probably do need to have your business materials/equipment insured. Consider where you'll be working from and what you'll be using, and make sure that these are added to your home contents insurance package.

Regarding personal indemnity and public liability insurances, some of the things you need to consider include:

1. Will you be working onsite for any clients?
2. Will clients or business-related people be visiting your premises?
3. Does your home contents insurance cover your office contents?
4. Do you offer any advice which could impact another business?
5. Could your services impact another business negatively?
6. Are you running any events?
7. Will you need public liability for any marketing initiatives? (e.g. expo/festival stands)
8. How is your business structured? Who is liable?

The frustrating thing is that you never know if someone will try to sue you at some stage in the future. Some people are very litigious and will cry out for a lawyer as soon as something doesn't work out for them. There is only so much that your agreement and your behaviour/standards can help – if someone wants to pursue legal action, you need to be ready.

Most VAs would be encouraged to have insurance based on their setup. You're running a business and offering services. It's all a risk. Did you know that anyone can sue you if they trip over at your home? And most people are not insured for this. So, if you do decide to arrange some insurance (which is tax deductible), then it will most likely cover you for all sorts of incidents that you would never have thought about before.

Also, remember that you can stuff things up without even realising it. We're always learning in business and being virtual we're relying heavily on technical programs which may fail us or our clients and claim indemnity. You don't want to be the one who takes the fall when things go wrong.

Your insurances and agreements need to form part of your contingency plan. Always look at what could go wrong (but not focusing solely on that all the time – it's not healthy!) and what the contingencies are that you can implement.

Several years ago, the business my husband and I were running together relied heavily on a hosting provider which was hacked. It had massive impacts on so many businesses offering hosting and website services, and we were one of them. We were lucky because we managed to hold onto our clients even though their services were seriously disrupted. Our agreements clearly stated that we would not be liable for service outages beyond our control, but what we focused on was what we could do to help each client during that stressful time. Partnering our determination to help our clients out along with our terms and conditions, allowed our business to survive when so many others fell over.

Had the problem been caused by us, we would need to have had the right insurance in place to pay out all of these clients who lost potential revenue and productivity. You never know what issue may arise or how it may eventuate – which is why insurance was invented in the first place.

Contingencies

Having contingencies in place, including insurance, is vital. You never know when you may become unwell or some other 'shit hits the fan'. So many sections of this book look at things you need to grow your business, and a lot impact your contingencies.

For example, networking, subcontracting, insurance, processes and procedures are all important so you can get through times when you're not able to support your clients.

While we don't want to focus on the negatives, it's important to think about what could go wrong (and what could go right – like taking a holiday!) and how that will be managed.

I have lost count of the number of times that VAs I know have had a disaster happen or been so close to disaster - hubby ends up in hospital, your kid breaks an arm at school, gastro strikes, you can't come back from holiday because of volcanic ash in the air stopping flights, your computer died or the internet/power went down, communication breakdowns, people being unethical – so many things can impact your service delivery. And what's the plan?

Apart from insurance, I recommend you connect and get to know some other great VAs. Get some business besties. Support each other and have a plan for when things are in disaster mode. If you want to have a team, make sure your team know what to do if something goes wrong. What's the 'fire plan'? Write it down, run through it and keep it updated.

Case study #5: Contingencies in action

Hanna Finlay, Off-site Reception

Hanna Finlay runs Off-site Reception which provides virtual reception services. As well as having a 'super awesome' in-house team, Hanna has an off-site team of VAs who are also trained in most of her client's needs.

At one point, they were unlucky enough to have a black-out in the office and couldn't get things back online. Because of her contingencies, Hanna was able to flip the phones over to the off-site team, therefore making sure the phones were still being covered.

Further to this, they now all run from laptops, and there is a designated phone that has backup internet for hot-spotting so that if they're ever stuck without power or internet, they can still function without issue.

Agreements

Your agreement needs to cover all aspects of your service delivery. As we explored earlier, your business IS unique, so your agreement needs to be customised to suit your set up and delivery, and the clients you're targeting.

Consider the elements of a business and what you might need to state in your agreement so that the business arrangement is clear to both you and your client from the very beginning. Sometimes issues arise, and personalities clash – consider all these possibilities and ensure that they're covered in your agreement.

An agreement should look at ensuring the confidence and security of all parties involved. It shouldn't just be a directive of all the things you expect from your client. It should include what the client can be expecting from you, too.

At all developmental stages of your agreement ask yourself, 'Would I sign this document?'. If you wouldn't sign the document if you put yourself in the shoes of your client, then it's not a fair and balanced agreement, and you need to modify it. An agreement should support both parties and ensure that both are looked after in all scenarios.

For example, if you're working on a retainer basis and you expect the client to provide a certain amount of notice before cancellation, it's only fair that the rule applies to you too if you wish to cancel the agreement. I had a client once who didn't want to provide notice, and I responded with, "That's fine, we can remove that, but we would also need to remove the section stating that I provide you with notice". He thought about that for a minute and promptly changed his mind. It was then that he realised that the agreement was to show that we're there to support each other, not that I want him to agree to a bunch of terms all in my favour.

Here are eight things that you should include in your agreement (huge thanks to Gary Horsman for letting us share these great points)

If you've been a solo freelancer for any significant stretch of time, you've probably learned the hard way that a work project can go horribly wrong. They turn out to be life lessons in the long run, but there are ways to protect yourself.

Working with bad projects or bad clients generally boils down to mismatched expectations and inadequate communication. Your best safeguard is to make sure you and your client are on the same page before any work has even begun using a Terms of Service Agreement, which essentially puts into clear, written language what you expect from your client and what they should expect from you.

By submitting a comprehensive Terms of Service Agreement to your client beforehand and having them return confirmation to agree to abide by your terms, you will be saving yourself (and your client) a lot of headaches down the road and avoiding the kind of surprises that can cause a project to get derailed.

1. **Billing structure.** What are your rates? Do you bill by the hour or by the project? This is important because it's usually one of the first three questions a new client will ask. Agree with the client what a final estimate includes and what will happen if changes are requested beyond the scope of the initial parameters of the project.

2. **Late payment.** Determine the grace period within which a client can submit their payment after the invoicing date. The standard practice is 30 days, but you can determine this according to your particular company. Also, spell out late fees and/or interest rates for late payments. This will give incentive to your clients to pay their invoices sooner than later.

3. **Interim charge caps.** I've known too many freelancers that have rung up large invoices for major projects adding up to thousands of dollars only to be shafted by deadbeat clients who walk away with your hard work. If you're working on a major project or are doing several smaller projects for one client that add up to major charges, put a cap on how much outstanding debt the client can carry.

I personally put a $500 cap on my clients so that when their total bill exceeds that amount, they will need to make an interim payment to bring it under or face work suspension. This will prevent clients from promising lots of high-paying business without delivering on their word. This is paramount when it comes to new clients, even those referred by people you trust.

You have the option to waive this cap if you have a long-standing relationship with a trusted client who pays on time and in full.

4. **Scheduling.** Can you service your clients twenty-four hours a day? Weekends? Holidays? You need to have a balanced life, which means you need to set hours that make sense with your lifestyle. Set appropriate hours when your clients can contact you and expect you to work. If you don't want to be woken by a panicking client at one in the morning, tell them specifically at what time your shop closes.

5. **No spec work allowed.** This is a controversial subject among many freelancers and prospective clients. The consensus for most is not to accept work on spec. Speculative work involves doing actual work with the hopes of impressing the client enough that they will provide further opportunities without any guarantee of payment or that you will retain rights over the work if it isn't paid for. It is bad practice to allow for this type of work with the extremely rare exception of once-in-a-lifetime opportunities. Your time and talent are

precious and shouldn't be doled out for free under any circumstance. Spell it out in the agreement: no spec work.

6. **Termination of services by client.** If you're a writer or a designer or another creative professional, and you're submitting a first draft to a client, and they are unsatisfied and want to end the project then and there saying something to the effect that your work does not meet their needs, they may be looking to get out of paying for the time you spent already, or worse, intending to steal your ideas for free. An honest client will pay for your time and move on to another freelancer. Otherwise, you've effectively just worked for spec and received a rejection. Set a minimum rate for work done that is immediately refused and where the client does not wish to allow you to continue.

    It should be stipulated that work that is refused by the client cannot be used in whole or in part. This may or may not be respected, but can be actionable as long as the client has agreed to this term and then subsequently violated it.

7. **Ownership rights.** Establish who owns the work after it has been completed and what rights the owner has to use or modify the final product. You may also want to consider retaining rights to utilise the work in a repertoire or portfolio for future promotion while the client retains all other major usage rights.

8. **Unforeseen or sudden termination of a project.** Most freelancers work on their own, so if some mishap, illness or accident occurs that makes it impossible to continue a project in progress, the client needs to know what protections they have. You may have to associate yourself with a backup freelancer who will agree to take over. Otherwise, you can make a provision where files or assets for a project are turned over to the client to be continued by someone else and billed for the work done up to that point.

Whatever you decide, let the client understand that however unlikely, hiring a single freelancer has certain risks and that there will be some compensation or provision made in case of a stoppage.

Most clients will act in good faith, so keep an open mind and be willing to negotiate in instances where there is disagreement. But by explicitly setting the terms in advance, potential disputes can be avoided, and you can focus on what's most important: doing great work.

***

Many business owners (including myself over the years!) fall into the trap of working with friends, family or people who are referred by someone they know, without putting agreements in place. This is the same as working with someone and not clearly stating and agreeing on expected outcomes. It's dangerous and can end badly.

The reason why this is so common is that:

1. People assume that friends or family will always be nice even if things go wrong;
2. It won't go wrong because we're friends, and
3. It can feel very uncomfortable to ask someone so familiar to you to sign an agreement.

What I recommend to people is that the agreement is in place because you want to stay friends. And to keep the relationship intact, you need to be clear about expectations, processes and contingencies. Ironically, things are more likely to go wrong without an agreement in place purely because those expectations have not been laid out and agreed to. So please – let friends and family know that you care by putting agreements in place.

Getting paid

One of the hardest things for many self-employed individuals is chasing money owed. You work so hard to build a rapport with the client, nurture the relationship and then bam – awkward territory.

When a client doesn't pay on time there are a few ways it can impact you:

1. Cash flow
2. Cost of time chasing

3. Feeling unappreciated = a blow to the confidence
4. Negative impact on the business-client relationship.

What can you do to reduce the impact of late and non-payers? The answer is to GET PAID!

Here are my top tips for getting paid by clients promptly:

Upfront payments

Upfront payments cost you less in administration, ensure that the job is paid for, and improves your cash flow. When you insist on upfront payments, you do need to remember to nurture the relationship and don't focus on it being based on mistrust. Having simple, clear processes for upfront payments can make this easy and non-confronting for clients. Upfront payments work well for projects and retainers. If your client has ad-hoc tasks on a regular basis and you won't start until you've received the outline, quoted and then received payment, this can hold things up. So, look at ways of streamlining your systems, so it's easy for clients to delegate work to you.

Agreements

An agreement should outline exactly what the payment terms are, all expectations and contingencies. Without an agreement in place things can become very uncomfortable very quickly as you resort to "he said/she said" evidence. Your agreement should support both parties and ensure that the process is streamlined and efficient.

Cease work

Your agreement should also state that when an account becomes overdue further work will be put on hold until the account is up to date. A client with important work that needs to be done will usually respond very quickly to this action. Threatening to stop work when it is not clearly outlined (and preferably verbally stated) before commencing work can impact the relationship. Make sure that you're always clear and friendly about the terms, so clients know exactly how it all works.

A credit agreement

A proper credit agreement will include referees from the clients' other suppliers and check for any bad debt history. The credit agreement will still state due dates, liabilities and the steps which will be taken should the account be outstanding.

Use a bookkeeper and a debt collector

Asking for money from clients can sometimes feel like the uncomfortable part of an otherwise great relationship. Outsourcing this component – from invoicing to 'chasing' – can separate you from the process and formalise the process somewhat. This method is often perceived as more 'professional' and an otherwise 'casual payer' may take more notice and action if they're dealing with someone else.

If you want more tips and guidance on collecting payments, I recommend you check out the Collect More app created by Paul Metcalf available on iTunes.

Myth buster: You shouldn't charge friends and family

Charging friends and family is hard. And once you offer something for free, it gets even harder to set boundaries around when billing should start if they want more help. As a strategy around this, I find that having a free initial consultation which also outlines costs moving forward is a good idea. For friends and family, you may offer a 10% discount (or something that still fits into your financial structure) across the services but be clear about anything that might fall outside the scope of this. And let them know that this is a special discount that you only offer friends and family.

You need to respect your services and understand your financials, no matter who you want to work with.

Some people have a blanket rule not to work with family or close friends. Instead, they refer them on to another quality provider instead as this avoids the 'working with family/friends trap' altogether. Working with family and friends can be so hard, so I recommend this. You may find that your family and friends' personalities are too close to your own and you lock horns as soon as business mode is applied. The odds of family or friends being your ideal client are slim!

Pricing

One of the first things a new VA asks is, 'What should I charge?'. This is an impossible question to answer without knowing a bunch of things about the service.

- How quickly and efficiently are you going to be easing the client's business pain?
- How good will the end outcome be?
- What is that worth to your ideal client?

The service is often mistaken for something like 'transcription' or 'website development' when in fact the service is so much more than that. The service is the whole experience and outcome for the client. You may have heard the concept of never being able to have something 'quick, cheap and good' – but you can pick two. It can be cheap and good, but it will not be quick. Or you can have quick and cheap, but it will not be good. What can people get from you?

What you can offer are quality processes and systems to make sure you're ticking at least 2 of those boxes. Ideally, you'd want your client to have a great outcome, quickly and at a good price for everyone involved – where you're getting paid what you're worth, and they see the value in what you deliver. The key to that is ensuring that buying from you is easy and stress-free for the client. So, it may not be cheap, but it's quick, good (I'd prefer it to be great!) and stress-free.

As with so many elements of your business, knowing as much as possible about your ideal client is going to make life easier. Your ideal client will see the value of what you offer and so will you.

There are calculators/spreadsheets you can use to calculate what you'd need to charge at a minimum to meet your financial goals based on expenses and time available to you. It's worth checking this and seeing whether what you want is going to be viable. Is that minimum amount aligned to the true value of what you offer?

You can download a useful spreadsheet in the Business Templates section at www.virtuallyyours.com.au.

You can do research and see what others are charging, but always be aware that their processes and method of delivery will impact their value. If they lack in this area and the delivery is not easy for the client, then they may be ticking the 'quick and cheap' boxes. Alternatively, they may have put a lot of effort into the whole experience for the client and the outcome – so they'd be ticking the good and quick boxes. Their pricing would be higher because of it.

Consider the effort you will be bringing to setting up a service that provides a stress-free experience for your client. Make sure you know whether your ideal client is seeking 'cheap and quick' or more of a 'high-end outcome and experience'.

There's a lot to consider when pricing. Who do you want to attract and can you deliver what they need in the best possible way? What is it worth to your ideal client? Will you be able to sustain and grow your business?

Don't price anything based on its value to YOU. When you're providing a service that you're great at, you'll rarely see the true value. If it's easy for you, you may find yourself undervaluing it. Always look at it from the end-user perspective. What's it worth to them?

When I did my calculations, I found that anything under $30 per hour was not worth doing, and even then, $30 an hour was never going to allow my business to grow. I couldn't subcontract effectively at that price, and I wasn't making much profit. Once you factor in expenses, it doesn't leave much.

Just because you're working from home and it's a service rather than a product doesn't mean you won't have plenty of expenses. Maintaining a computer (monitor, mouse, keyboard), fast internet, software programs, insurance, stationery, training, networking, travel, printing, mentoring etc. all add up. And they can add up very quickly. I've also found that because my husband and I both work from home we have higher electricity and heating costs and we tend to eat what we want all day long which can be expensive too!

Not all your hours will be billable, so you need to factor that in too. Not to mention no one will pay you when you are sick or on holidays. And superannuation and tax - who is paying that?

All of these are why it's important to offer a high quality streamlined service to the clients who need and value it most, so you can charge what you need to, to not only pay all of those bills but to then make a profit as well.

Always walk a mile in your client's shoes. Find out what their goals are for the year. See how you can help them. See where you fit in and how you can make your client think, "Wow - where would I be without my VA?"

Packaging – Dos and don'ts

Packages are important for many VAs but don't stress if it's not for you. Packages can be valuable because they clarify the outcomes and benefits to the client, streamline your processes and allow you to charge for outcomes rather than hours.

When referring to packaging, I am not talking about packaging hours. When you're talking about packaging hours, it is more of a retainer type of situation that isn't outcome based and is still capped. What people tend to do when they package hours is they give discounts, so they're not reaping any benefit from the fact that they're packaging. The only thing they're getting is consistency, but they're getting that at a sacrifice of income. They also tend to find they're working with clients who are focused on time rather than an outcome which is not ideal for them or the client. Worrying about how much time your VA has or hasn't spent is not helpful for the client. If they know what the outcome is, irrelevant of the time spent, then they can relax about the hours.

With outcome-based packages, one benefit is that it's easier to communicate to your client what they're getting in return for their investment.

Whereas if you're going to be telling them that you're going to be delivering stuff, but the focus is on the hours, it's less tangible and very, very hard for people to get their heads around.

When we're looking at outcomes, we're looking at things like:

- Managing CRM
- E-newsletters

- Websites
- Logo creation
- Social media management
- Content management

So, you win some, and you lose some? Yes, but the way you win more is to have a good client filter, client intake process and clear guidelines and clear processes - reducing the chance of having a client or a job that drags out. If you have jobs that are dragging out, the hours are getting ridiculous, and you find you're working for $5 an hour, then you need to fix that communication and expectation process. Not just the price, not just outcome but the process as it's not working.

Therefore, packaging processes and communication are going to be massive.

Benefits of packaging

Let's say that you manage your client's phone and CRM. Make sure you consider what is going to impact you regarding your involvement in it, their involvement and their pain points when determining the package price. If they have 2000 addresses in their CRM that they're not doing anything with, and phone calls are ringing out, then giving them two hours support means nothing to them. However, saying, "I will make sure those 2000 people are going to get a touch point either by a newsletter or an SMS every week or month, and I'll ensure a prompt response to all enquiries", is more tangible.

You'll help your client:

- Stay in the forefront of their prospects minds
- Share their message, product, events, etc. to key people
- Make the most of their database
- Support and provide customer care to their database
- Avoid losing leads or existing clients
- Reduce the number of interruptions they may have previously had when managing their client base
- Provide reports, so the client knows what areas they need to build on, what's working and what isn't

Sometimes working out the benefits is hard for you because it's your service and you're too close to the project. Having a chat with a copywriter can help you come up with a message that is clear and succinct and on brand – communicating the benefits to the ideal client.

Remember with packages that you need to set limits on what is included and what is outside of the agreed scope. Useful words here are "up to". For example, "up to 4 newsletters per month". This helps you when there are factors outside of your control that result in fewer issues being sent out. For example, the client doesn't provide the information needed, or you both agree that you don't need one during a certain period. The reduced number of newsletters won't affect the package rate, but you'll both need to agree on those conditions before they occur.

If I have booked you in for a set package, there are other benefits to me aside from those obvious deliverables.

- I can budget because I know what it's going to cost me every month
- We can plan the year ahead and work out when the peak periods and quiet periods are and average out the cost to cover it
- I can measure what is working and what isn't
- I know that you've set that time aside to deliver those outcomes
- I know that you've got a backup plan to deliver those outcomes even if you're sick or away (make sure you have!)
- I'll have consistent outcomes
- You'll be there for the long-term and become part of the team – that is another benefit

You might end up having a month that is completely crazy, and you might have a month that is quiet where nothing is happening, but you'd still charge the same amount, and you want it to average out across the year.

This budget is helping the client, and the budget is helping you too - it goes two ways.

When you do this sort of thing with them in advance, you know what their workload is going to be like, and they've got a package, then they also know that you're going to be available as you have already planned to be available during those peak periods. This is a big thing for the client because neither of you wants to get to June and then have them say, "I have this huge event next month, alright VA this is what we are going to be doing" and you respond with, "Well actually, I am going away, or I am already booked up." Disaster.

Planning so that your package can be delivered across the year is a massive benefit to all parties.

With packages which are one-offs such as system setups, you'd still let them know what the duration of the project will be (not the number of hours worked), and what the outcomes are.

When you start doing ongoing packages, it's important that you have some contingencies in place. You may be going away, you may get sick, you may break a leg, you may have something happen with a family member, you may have a new opportunity come up or another client job, or everything might just hit the fan. Whatever it is, you need to have contingencies in place to be offering packages.

TIP: If you know who your ideal client is, talk to them when you're creating your package and make sure that it's easing their pain.

Myth Buster: You need to give your clients a résumé

BUSTED!

ré·su·mé n. A brief account of one's professional or work experience and qualifications, often submitted with an employment application.

In business, it can sometimes be hard for both the VA and the client to see the relationship as something other than an employee/employer partnership. This is simply because, in the past, that's the only way it was done. No one ever hired another business owner to do their admin. You hired a secretary. I mean goodness – wouldn't it be INSANE to let another business owner see your business undies...?

The lines get a little blurrier these days when we look at how much broader the term 'Virtual Assistant' has become. It's gone from secretarial to all types of business support services. The main criteria being that the service is for businesses, and it's done off-site. So now there are VAs who could just as accurately refer to themselves as bookkeepers, web developers, writers, consultants or graphic designers.

It would feel weird to ask your bookkeeper or accountant for their resume – after all, they aren't becoming your employee. But you would be wise to seek some testimonials and find out what their qualifications are. Websites, brochures and of course, word of mouth are great for these.

A VA, in this sense, is no different.

If you want to work with a VA and you want to see a resume, I believe you're setting up a false relationship. And the VAs that respond with a resume may not have the right mindset to support you most appropriately.

Stay with me.

You go to someone and say you need to see their resume. In your mind, you want someone who:

- Is under you
- Can take direction and be there for you when you need them
- Accepts the rate that you set

When you find someone who is ok with that, you may find that they're still in the employee mindset and you discover:

- They aren't confident enough to provide you with guidance and ideas that will grow your business
- They aren't ready to take full responsibility for their own, let alone your, business
- They rely on you to keep them going.

And if you are paying a low rate, why shouldn't they?

New VAs need time to learn how to run a business – I don't question that. But they shouldn't do it by holding onto the employee mindset.

VAs are service providers. They are self-employed, and that means:

- They run their own business
- They must understand business well to survive
- They must bring more money in than goes out
- They can't put all their eggs in one basket
- They must pay taxes
- They are responsible for their growth, which is usually because of their client's growth – just like an accountant, a designer, a lawyer or a plumber

For the client, this also means:

- They can use their services as you need them
- They are not responsible for putting food on their table
- They don't pay super, annual leave, WorkCover, sick leave or for time not used
- They can plan and budget better
- They will have access to someone who will always be on top of the latest tools and resources – and not at their expense – just like an accountant, a designer, a lawyer or a plumber, although in this case you also get a sidekick who 'gets' business and is invested in your success

In summary – a résumé is all very nice, but it sets up the mindset and intent of the relationship. If you start giving out resumes as a VA, you'll tell your clients that you're still in an employee mindset. This can cause all sorts of issues when those lines are blurred.

MARKETING

✱✱✱

I received an email from a VA who has been running her business for almost a year, and she has only secured one client at that time. She is feeling like she is struggling to secure additional clients and it's stressing her out.

She told me that she was attending networking events (excellent!), giving her business cards out to local businesses and introducing herself and that she had created a website, ensuring it ranks well on Google.

While these were all good, they still left me with a lot of questions which I'll pose to you here. Hopefully, you will have solid answers to these questions when considering your business marketing.

Networking

1. When networking, are you targeting events/locations where your ideal client would most likely be? Or are

you just attending events where everyone is the same as you?

2. How do you introduce yourself to others at the event so that they can see and feel how you could work in with their business and solve their problems?

3. Are you presenting yourself to appeal to your market? (Your clothing, language and body language)

4. How do you follow up with people you've met at networking events?

5. Do you have a clear objective when attending networking events?

6. Are you using networking only to find clients, or are you also looking for a business community? (recommended)

There is nothing worse than someone flittering around a networking event handing out business cards. I've seen it before, and I've seen the receivers of those cards put them straight into the bin. Networking is for networking, not littering. Any time you hand your card to someone, it should be because they've asked for it. People won't ask for your card until they are interested in learning more about you and potentially contacting you or referring someone to you. To achieve this, you need to do one important thing; ask and listen.

Learn about people. Care about them and what they do. Ask questions and listen to the answers. It's a well-used expression but true, that "all things being equal, people do business with people who they know, like and trust" (Bob

Burg).

This knowing, liking and trusting is only going to be achieved by getting to know someone, finding out about them and determining that you're a good match.

After a networking event do you usually know which contacts would be useful to follow up with and why? Some reasons why you'd want to follow up may include:

Because they were:

1. someone you'd like to learn more from,
2. someone you'd like to work with,
3. someone you'd like to refer someone else to,
4. a great person and you want to stay in touch!

Whatever the reason, do you have a process for following up? I highly suggest writing something on their card (if you can) to help you remember who they were and why you wanted to connect with them.

Please try to avoid contacting people to 'pick their brain'. Catching up for a coffee or a Skype chat is great, but please explain what it is you want to achieve from that connection. People can feel very wary about catching up with someone who is vague about why they want to catch up because there are a few people out there who arrange a catch up simply to pitch their services and try to sell, sell, sell . Always respect the time of the person you want to connect with. If you clicked and want to be friends, then it's pretty simple, and you do that. If you think you could collaborate – say so. If you want to learn more about their business – say so. If you want to tell them more about your business – stop now and don't continue unless they've clearly stated that they want to know more about you. If you want to ask them for advice – at least offer to buy them lunch. Appreciate the knowledge they would be sharing with you. Most people charge for consulting time, so don't assume you can get all their wisdom for free!

Networking is no longer just face to face. So much of our networking is now online on social platforms like Facebook, LinkedIn, Twitter and even Instagram. Each of these platforms has different missions, and the communication within them changes from platform to platform. Twitter, for example, is very fast paced with short messages. Facebook is often much more casual and relaxed while LinkedIn can be rather formal and seen as an online business platform more than a social platform. Platforms like Instagram and Pinterest are very visual and use pictures to grab attention and communicate. Knowing which of the platforms are going to be most useful for you will help you avoid spending time on one that won't benefit you or your business. When you understand who your ideal client is, you'll usually be able to get an idea on which of the platforms they're most likely going to be spending their time on. And of course, that's where you'll need to network too.

One of the biggest issues with online networking is

that many people will say things online that they would never (and should never) say in person. The term 'keyboard warrior' refers to people who are tough and aggressive online because it's much easier to do so from behind your keyboard. When networking online, you always need to assess what you say and determine whether it is aligned with your brand before posting/submitting it. Ask yourself: 'Is it useful, is it kind and is it fair?'

You'll also find a lot of 'trolls' on social media. People who pick fights and make controversial comments (some that are completely horrific) just to get a response. It can be hard to maintain your control and dignity with trolls and keyboard warriors all over the place, but at the end of the day, you always need to remember that everything you say online can impact you. Not everything that others say online is a big deal – but what YOU say, is. So, as they say, 'don't feed the trolls' and always network online professionally. Before responding ask yourself "will my comment genuinely help anyone?".

If you have a social media page, you may come across these types who comment on your posts or who leave bad reviews. The way you respond is very important. In some cases, you can block and delete a comment or a review. This is recommended if the comment is horrible and irrelevant. But if someone disagrees with you or isn't happy with your service, don't automatically delete or get defensive. An intelligent, compassionate and non-emotive response will usually serve you well. Most people know that it's not the mistake that we judge, but the way in which you respond to it. There are some cases online where businesses such as restaurants or hotels have responded aggressively to bad reviews, and those responses have gone 'viral'. A viral post is something that has been shared, copied and spread across several social platforms. Going viral means that a post has generated a great deal of attention in the form of a high number of views, likes, shares and comments.

When something negative goes viral, it can severely impact your business brand. However, many clever responses to bad reviews or nasty/silly comments have also gone viral, and these have instead impacted those businesses positively.

Just like face to face networking, online networking should not involve you selling your services at every opportunity. Social media is meant to be social. It's about building relationships and in time, building that know-like-trust factor. On LinkedIn and Facebook, you can participate in groups, creating new topics or responding to existing topics. People who post promotions all the time instead of getting to know other group members are often ignored or banned and deleted. It's draining for others to hop onto a social media platform and be bombarded with ads. Make sure you follow the same rules of face to face networking when you are networking online.

Some people also participate in conversations on blog

posts and website forums. Please treat these the same as above and always keep your comments relevant to the original post. You wouldn't join a group of people chatting at a networking event and butt in with a completely new topic direction – so don't do that online either.

Branding

Your brand is your business personality. Your business should never be bipolar or schizophrenic – it needs to be consistent. It can be consistently straight-laced and serious, or consistently fun and quirky. But it needs to be consistent across the board.

Does your networking presence, your business card, logo, writing, messages, communication and delivery all align with your brand? Are they recognisable across the board? Are they consistent?

People who specialise in marketing know that buyers want to feel confident that they know who they are buying from and what they are buying. This is why franchises are so strict with their branding. If a franchisee does their own thing and it doesn't align with the franchise's personality (brand), then it creates confusion and uncertainty, which can affect client confidence and as a result, sales.

A couple of years ago there was a JB Hi-Fi franchise that discriminated against a young man with Down Syndrome. There was a lot of negative publicity and public outcry.

The other franchisees would have been affected by the actions of this franchisee, who gave the impression that this brand allows discrimination. Every activity that represents the business is an element of the brand, and the brand is responsible for creating confidence.

Customers need to feel they know what they're getting when they visit a business. Uncertainty can make people feel uncomfortable and especially in a service-based industry such as the VA Industry; clients must feel that the service is going to be reliable and trustworthy.

So what message does your brand send? What are the emotions and thoughts you want your customers to experience when they see or work with you? How will you achieve that consistently?

Importantly, your brand needs to resonate with your ideal client. Your brand can be very beautiful and classy, but if your ideal client doesn't resonate with that, then it won't work for you. Think about what your ideal client likes. What they want to feel. What their fears are. Does your brand give them confidence that you can ease their fears and business pains?

When considering the areas we've already explored (such as services, target market, your uniqueness, networking and your website), how will you set these up and use these to communicate a consistent and converting brand? The way you speak in your emails, on social media, on your website, on your phone and messaging services should all align with your brand ethos.

Brand specialists have a good eye for consistency (yes, we use that word a lot when talking about branding) and connecting with your ideal client. They understand that the colours you use, the tone and words in your writing, the imagery and the way you deliver your services, must all be working together to provide solutions to your ideal client. Branding is not something you should skim over but it can be something that evolves. It should be part of your ongoing business development and stay valuable and relevant to your ideal client (who may also evolve).

Your website

Your website is like an online business card and brochure but can do so much more. With the right set up, your website should be found by the right people, give them the information they want and need before they decide to purchase from you and guide them to the next steps so they can purchase from you.

Some of the things to consider when evaluating or setting up your website include:

1. If you're directing people to your website, what do they see when they visit your website? Does it clearly explain

how you can solve their problems?

2. Do you have a call to action? (something on the site that tells the visitor what you want them to do. I.e. call you, subscribe, buy now, download)

3. Is it easy for them to take this action?

4. How long do people tend to stay on your site when they do visit? (Use Google Analytics to check this)

5. Which pages do they view?

6. When considering Search Engine Optimisation (SEO), what words/phrases are you optimised for? Are they the words/phrases your ideal client would use?

7. When listed on Google, what information about you is shown before they even click on your link?

Don't settle for a website that you aren't proud of. There is nothing worse than handing out your business card and saying, "Please ignore how my site looks – it's a work in progress!". I know, I've been there. It's embarrassing. Get it fixed!

With your business being virtual, your website is your shop front. You wouldn't set up a shop with a hideous shop front, so why do that with your website? And if website development isn't your thing – outsource it.

When someone visits your site, does it guide them and educate them? Does it inspire action?

This isn't always easy to achieve and is often in itself an

evolving project. But if you aren't sure how to do this, it's worth working with someone who understands marketing and can help you connect with your ideal client.

It's obvious that your website should look good – be clean and professional, have smart modern appeal and be free of spelling or grammar errors. But you should also ensure that it takes your prospects from A (might consider buying from you) to B (wanting to buy from you and knowing how and why to buy from you). Often a prospect won't buy from you because there is a gap for them around what it is you offer or how you offer it. They may not know what they need to do to use your services. Consider the questions a prospect would normally ask you if they know nothing, or very little, about how to use a Virtual Assistant, and make sure those questions are answered on your site. Remember that as a Virtual Assistant, you are asking them to trust you to help them with their business. Use your website to reinforce that feeling of trust in your capabilities and your ethics. They need to know that working with you will be safe and beneficial. They need to know that they can trust you with their business.

Your website is only useful if it's found. Make sure you have strategies in place to maintain a good ranking on Google and ensure people who connect with you on social media platforms or at networking events can find your site easily. Always list your website address on your social media pages, your business card and your email signature – make it easy to find and then make it useful to read.

Now, this may sound counterintuitive but don't set up your website before you've worked out what service you are offering, to who and how. Be clear on who you want to have visiting your site and what you want them to do. Have a strategy in place. It's ok to not have a website for a little while as you work this out. So many people spend all of their startup dollars on a new website when they don't know what they want it to do. Spend the money on working out who, why, and how – and you won't have to recreate your website a few months down the track.

Copyright

Way too often, I've seen people setting up a VA business and naming it without checking the Trademark Register for conflicts. It's a bug-bear of mine that when they register a business name, for the Australian Securities and Investments Commission (ASIC) anyway, they tick a little box confirming that they understand that:

Registering a business name does not protect you against third party claims for trademark infringement.

To ensure your proposed business name doesn't infringe on an existing registered trademark, you should use IP Australia's Australian Trade Mark Search to search for existing trademarks.

They then spend time and effort developing all their

branding only to find that someone else has trademarked it and is not happy that it's been copied. Then they need to start all over again. I find it frustrating as it makes extra work for the business owners who have the trademarks because they have to police and enforce it.

Website and advertising wording is another area where people get copied. We all know it's hard to explain our services and products, so get a copywriter to help you. Don't copy and paste (and then do a few 'tweaks') from other people's sites. It's not cool.

Over the years I've also seen evidence of people ripping off and copying entire training programs – replicating the content, the delivery and even sometimes the branding! It's a surefire way to get yourself into legal strife and to ensure you won't be trusted by other business owners ever again.

A couple of years ago a business set themselves up with an almost identical name to mine, working in the same industry and country. When I first saw her promotions on Facebook, I did a double-take thinking they were my own! Yes, the name was slightly different, but the colouring and the service were way too close for comfort, and yes, they breached my trademark. People had reported to me that they'd been confused about whether it was my business or not and I could see some of my friends had 'liked' the page thinking it was mine! This was enough for me to contact an Intellectual Property lawyer to see what I could do.

Initially, I approached the business owner and let her know that there was a breach and I'd appreciate if she changed her business name and branding. She told me to get stuffed and that I didn't have a 'leg to stand on'. She arrogantly informed me that her 'Barrister friend" told her she was well within her rights. To this day I wonder if her friend was a coffee master rather than legal. Thankfully my lawyer disagreed. The copycat also gave me a sob story about a sick mother, claiming that I was cruel for challenging her seeing as she was going through this personal tragedy. She used every trick in the book to get me to back off, but she was using my brand reputation to jump-start her own.

My lawyer issued her with a cease and desist notice and billed her for my legal fees. I had warned the business owner that this was what would happen, but she laughed at me. She soon turned incredibly angry when she was contacted by my lawyer. Funnily enough, she did change her branding very quickly as the threat of more penalties loomed. She didn't want to pay the legal fees (surprise surprise), but with the help of a great debt collector, I managed to get her to pay most of those legal fees. I've since seen her copying other business owners and I'm shocked she is still in the business arena. I'm sure she'll end up on A Current Affair one day!

With each story I hear of her copying someone, I see her rebranding and starting again. She must have spent countless hours rebuilding and recopying different business owners over the years, and I have no idea how that could ever be profitable for her. I also don't know how she sleeps at night.

The business world is smaller than people think. People know people. And word can travel fast. You may find yourself protected by privacy laws to a point – people won't want to name and shame you for fear of slander claims – but behind closed doors, they will let their peers know who to trust and who to avoid. Be someone who can be trusted and build your unique offering.

Marketing

Consider:

- Where are you promoting your business?
- Is that promotion likely to be found and viewed by your ideal client?
- Do you measure your results?
- Do you have a strategic plan?

Marketing is all about getting people who need your services to notice your services. Without a strong marketing strategy, you could have a great idea that never gets off the ground.

The most important thing about marketing is that it's seen by and resonates with your ideal client. Everything you write, say or do, should be aimed at that ideal client. This means your promotions need to be where your ideal client will see them, at a time when your ideal client would see them, and allow action in a way that your ideal client would want to and can take action.

What's your plan? Without knowing who your ideal client is (and this will often evolve based on experience and research), you are just throwing brochures into the wind and hoping one hits the right person on the head.

Always practice the *6 Ps of marketing:*

- Product
- Price
- Promotion
- Place
- Process
- People.

Product

Having a strong and clear service offering helps reduce confusion and resistance from your clients. By understanding your ideal client, you can create a set of services or packages that solve your client's business woes.

Price

The price needs to ensure your business remains profitable and competitive. You need to consider all of the expenses associated with the development and maintenance of the service, including time spent developing the concept, delivery methods, and logistics. The final price needs to be something your ideal client will be willing to pay. If there is a misalignment, you may need to reassess the price or the target market.

Promotion

The places we network are often the places we run our promotions. It's important to have a good mix of communication types when networking both online and face to face. If you are networking in either format and spend the whole time talking about yourself and your services, people will get bored quickly and move on. This method does not build the 'know, like and trust factor'. People want to talk about themselves – not about you. And while you might want to talk about yourself too, you need to ensure a balanced mix. As with any relationship building, we take turns; we talk, we listen, we ask questions – and not always in that order. Remember, you have one mouth and two ears for a reason – you need to listen twice as much as you talk.

Assuming you have a good balance in place, your promotions need to serve a purpose. Have a strategy that can be measured. There's no point running a promotion on Facebook that sends people to your website if you don't have something in place that then directs them on to the next step or the destination you want them to reach. Your promotions should have inbuilt filters, so only the right sort of people respond to them and follow the steps. There are lots of tools and resources you can use to target and measure social media marketing, and there are a few VAs who specialise in this area. It may be worth outsourcing some of your marketing strategies to them as it can be quite technical.

Sponsorship, collaboration or being a guest speaker are other ways you can promote your services. For each of these, you need to ensure that the audience for that activity aligns with your target market. As a website developer, you may feel that presenting to a group of tradespeople would be a waste of time, but to a VA specialising in supporting tradies with appointment management and reception, this would be the perfect place to be.

It can be hard at times to think of places where you can promote your business so here is a short list to get you thinking:

- Contests
- Social media
- Giveaways / trials
- Affiliate or reward systems
- Causes and charities
- Promotional gifts
- Expo / conference tables
- Speaking gigs
- Surveys.

Place

Where will people be able to purchase your service: online, face to face, phone, or email? What is the journey like for them from the initial thought to hire a VA through to signing up with you?

Process

Having a service-based business means having strong processes in place. Understand the journey for your client and how you'll ease their pain. Ensure your processes, as much as possible, don't add stress or extra work for your client (unless that extra work reaps a great return on investment).

People

The people in your business will be your team, your stakeholders, and clients. They all need to be on the same page and understand your brand mission and processes. Clarity around your brand mission will help them promote your business in the way you want, and identify the right sort of people you want to be supporting and working with. When your team understand your brand mission, they can see opportunities that are a good fit for you and help direct your business towards that mission.

Responding to jobleads

Seven questions you must ask when responding to leads if you want to succeed

Guess what? Setting up your business and telling people you exist just ain't gonna cut it. Sorry to be the bearer of bad news but you can't just 'build it, and they will come'. But there are some really important things you need to remember to ensure that you're not losing out on opportunities for your business, and instead, are securing the clients you want. How are you responding to leads?

In today's day and age, we all have access to a huge number of resources – it's so easy to 'google' something, email a forum, post on social media or check with a colleague. If you need business support, you'll get a huge number of responses. But the quality of those responses can leave much to be desired. Assumptions, laziness, arrogance, and misleading are words that I would use to describe some of the responses that you can get when you call out for a resource these days.

One of the main things I see people doing is responding to calls for help with a simple "yeah I want the job" type of response. Has that ever worked for you?

As a visual person, I liken this to someone at the bottom of a well calling for help.

"Hello up there! I need help! Can you help me?"

For my story, let's say there are three people at the top of the well. One person lets the person in the well know they are there and that they could help.

"Hello down there! I could help you!" they say as they resume reading their book on a lounge chair under an umbrella, sipping a cool ice glass of water with lemon and mint – certain that the helpless well victim will reply with:

"Oh yes, please! I want YOU! What else can I do to get you to help me? I'm ALL yours! Hooray!"

The second person calls down:

"Hey there! I can help you out too. I have all the rope ladder building skills you need – visit my website for more details!".

They might even throw down an iPad so the victim can do their homework. So thoughtful.

The third person throws down a rope ladder as they ask questions like:

"Can you climb? Is it the top of the well that you wish to reach? What are you trying to achieve?"

Only the third person, who has taken the initiative, asked some questions and showcased their ability to help, will find out that the person in the well needs a torch so that they can keep exploring and developing this exciting well in which they've found themselves. Person number three can then develop a fabulous tailored proposal for the person in the well and inspire their new client to always come straight to them when they need some extra light.

Which person are you? How can you be person number three? If someone says they need support, ask questions.

Ask the PROSPECT:

1. Is my interpretation of your needs correct?
2. Can you clarify these gaps for me, so I am clear on what you need?

Ask YOURSELF:

3. Can I see what it is that the prospect is asking for?
4. Does this sound like something that I can and want to do?
5. How can I provide useful succinct information and examples to the client to make their decision-making process as easy as possible?
6. If the job is not a good fit for me can I suggest alternative resources for them that/who COULD assist them?
7. Could my involvement here help me learn something or help build a relationship?

Don't look at all the questions that are asked of you as dollar signs. Sometimes you can learn from this discussion with the prospect and build a relationship.

Today I asked a Facebook group for some support around business reporting. My question started off deliberately vague, but I was happy to see that some business owners contacted me directly to clarify what my needs were. These business owners wanted to help in some way – even if it wasn't going to give them the job at the end of the day. They genuinely wanted to help, and this instantly helps build rapport and confidence. They made useful suggestions and offered to keep an eye out for additional solutions to help ease my pain. Bingo!

Alternatively, a peer of mine asked a business support question in the same arena and was only contacted by people who wanted her needs to be moulded into what they wanted to offer. She knew what the parameters were that she needed to have met, but the people responding did NOT consider the 7 points above. They only looked at point 4 and failed to address the rest. Instead, their list of points looked more like:

Does this task/job sound like something that I can and want to learn more about?

Hmm, almost.

Ask the client if they can modify their needs to meet what I'd like to offer.

Suggest how and why the client should do this.

The prospect found this presumptuous, as those responding didn't think to ask first if she had considered the alternatives before they started trying to convince her that their solution and modification was the way to go. They wasted her time and their own so there were no winners.

There are times when the prospect is looking for ideas and potential scenarios – but unless they have specified that in their call for assistance, you shouldn't assume it. If anything is unclear – ask first, suggest later. Do your homework. Don't just show up and expect people to bend backwards and mould their needs to yours so that they can have the pleasure of working with you.

If you see a call for help or a joblead and you think – yes this sounds good for me to follow up - the first thing you need to do is some research. Google them. You'll have at least a name and usually a business name to start with, or even an email address. Some people don't realise that for most businesses, the website address and the email address have the same address in them. So my email is rosie@virtuallyyours.com.au – the first thing you'd do is visit www.virtuallyyours.com.au and see if that's my website. It is!

You'd then have a look around and learn what you can. You'll most likely notice social media icons, so I recommend you click on those next and see what else you can learn about this business.

Try to identify their:

- Values
- Brand mission

- Target market
- Product or service

See if you can identify any areas for improvement. Write a list of questions you have about their business that still hasn't been answered. See whether they look like they may be a good match to your avatar. A client onboarding checklist is very useful for this process .

Googling them is a good idea too – sometimes you may find that there is information about them online that doesn't align with your values, and you may use this information to decide whether you want to contact them to discuss the job further.

Once you've done some research, you should contact them. By phone is great but if they've given clear instructions that they want you to email them or private message them rather than calling – make sure you do that.

When you connect, let them know what you understand about the role and ask any questions you have. Let them know that you've looked them up and it's always worth highlighting anything you particularly liked about what you discovered. The initial contact is a two-way interview to see if you both want to discuss the role further. If so, follow up the call with an email outlining what you've discussed and what needs to happen next. Where possible, line up a face-to-face meeting – even if it's online using a program like Skype.

Once you've lined up a meeting (and if you're communicating about meeting dates via email, make it easy by using a scheduling software like Acuity or Calendly) write up an agenda and set a timeframe around the meeting length. Always be clear about the duration of the meeting, that it is complimentary, and when you need to start charging for your time – you don't want to sit there having a free 2-hour meeting!

In the meeting, hopefully, you can learn even more about what they're trying to achieve and how you can fit into that and help them get from A to B. Think about your future together and how it could work, what it would look like, what you could achieve, and be taking note whether you would communicate well together. You'd want to leave the meeting with a clear plan of what you both need to do next and the timelines associated with each activity.

The first task should be to draft up an agreement for both parties and get that signed. Never skip this step!

If you feel that it's not a good role for you, then you can say, "Look, you know I love what you're doing, but I feel like it is probably not going to work with us because of (whatever)". If you feel it is appropriate to re-direct them onto someone else. If not just thank them for their time and on you go.

If you're keen to work with the client and they've expressed the same you might say something along the lines of, "This sounds fantastic, and I am keen to move forward. What I'll be doing now is sending through an agreement outlining what we've just said so that it is in writing for you along with my privacy confidentiality policy. I'll send that by (date). Please, have a read and then confirm via email that you're happy to go ahead. After that what we'll do to get the ball rolling is.... (fill the blank)."

If the client isn't quite sure about going ahead yet, you can say, "That's fantastic for today. I know you still have more things to think about and other people you want to chat to. Would it be okay for me to give you a call in (2 or 3 days) to follow up and see where you're at with that and will take it from there?" You want to obtain permission to keep the ball rolling in a way that is non-threatening and supportive.

The more that you leave things open to interpretation the more it can go off track or get forgotten or becomes too hard for the client. Guide the relationship as best you can to make it easy for them, and it makes it easy for you as well.

How do you start on the right foot with your clients?

Meeting and chatting with a prospective client can be an intimidating or scary venture. Many VAs worry a lot about this part of the business. That first meeting and the steps you take before, during and after it can make or break your business relationship.

It's important to know how you want your business to run. What your goals are, how you want to work, when you want to work and how much money you want to earn. Being clear on your objectives helps you work out the smartest and easiest strategies moving forward with finding, securing and maintaining clients – the right clients.

Here are my seven tips for starting off on the right foot with your clients:

1. **Make it easy for them.** If you know who you want to work with, you should know how they communicate, what their pain points are, and how you can ease them. Use this knowledge to make finding and selecting you easy for your clients. Whenever I see someone respond to a call out for help with something like, "I can help – PM me", I cringe. I highly doubt their ideal client loves researching more about VAs while the work they need help with remains undone.

    Answer their questions, provide useful resources, arrange a time and location (F2F or virtual) to meet and have a chat. Use calendar booking software to make this easy.

2. **Do your research.** From the moment you're contacted by a prospect to the moment your meeting starts, make it a priority to learn what you can about them. Not only so you can address their needs better, but so you can also ascertain whether they'd be a good client for you.

If they aren't – make sure you don't waste your time holding a meeting with them. Not all prospects will end up clients, but you may find some become great friends, mentors, resources or referrers, so don't discount them if they could fit into your business in another way. However, make sure you are upfront about where you stand and don't lead them on thinking you'd be able to help them with their VA needs. You can always refer them to someone else.

3. **Set an agenda.** When you get to the meeting stage, having a basic agenda will help guide the conversation, ensure all questions are answered and avoid wasting yours and your prospects valuable time. The agenda should also include setting out a plan following the meeting, so you don't walk away from the meeting unsure of what step you're meant to take next. Know who is going to do what and by when.

4. **Follow up.** Do what you said you would do and make sure the conversation keeps going. Give the client the confidence to know that the job is in hand and their life will soon be easier. Follow up using the agreed method of communication that works best for both you and the client. Where appropriate, guide the client in the processes and activities that need to be undertaken to achieve their goals.

5. **Have an agreement in writing.** Always, always, always put your terms and conditions in writing. No

matter how you feel about your client (and this goes for subcontractors too), you need to put everything in writing. Any person or business that you collaborate or work with should have an agreement in place. Agreements can feel like a real downer – they seem too formal and not 'fun' and it can be very easy just to say, 'We'll be ok – I trust them, and they trust me." Famous last words. Not one person who has broken your trust has said that was what they were going to do. That's why it's a breach of trust. You simply never know what could happen. Always get everything that's important and relevant in writing.

6. **Stay connected and always deliver.** It's not uncommon for a business relationship to start to lose its novelty and shine and for the people working together to start to feel less excited about it. If this could happen or is happening, it's your responsibility to find a way to keep it important and interesting for you. When the novelty wears off, and the shine has waned, you may find yourself dropping the ball a bit, letting things slide and no longer putting effort into 'wowing' your client. Keeping a client is what makes a successful business. Happy, ongoing clients make a business thrive. Once you've secured the client – your job is to get the job done and continually wow the client. Never forget this.

    Regular meetings, goal setting, calendar planning etc. can keep you both excited and inspired and make sure you keep working on those common goals.

7. **Get and give feedback.** Make sure you know whether the work you're delivering and the timelines and method of delivery, are making your client happy and achieving the results you're aiming for. Ask for feedback and utilise the feedback to keep growing and improving. On the flip side, if there are things your client could be doing to make things work better, quicker or more smoothly, let them know. Work together to keep improving.

If you remind yourself daily of these 7 key points, you'll be able to ensure that you're attracting the right clients and keeping them. Working as a successful Virtual Contractor requires clarity, communication, dedication and a passion for ongoing improvement. Make these a staple in your business processes to avoid the pitfalls of attracting the wrong clients, not securing the right clients or losing the best clients.

Here are a few things extra tips to be an awesome VA:

- Always keep your client in the loop. Respond promptly (not out of business hours unless it's an emergency) and keep them updated so they can avoid wondering what's happening.
- Always remember and respect how hard it can be to let go.
- Don't do everything yourself – practice what you preach and get help in areas you aren't strong in or don't have time for.

- Always be honest.

- Don't compete based on your rates – compete on quality.

- Never forget why you wanted to do this in the first place.

- Set goals or 'desired outcomes' you want to achieve so you can keep growing and stay inspired.

- Mix things up if you feel you need to – you're in control of your business direction.

At the end of this book, I've included my 'Client: wow!' checklist. You can use it for each client to ensure you're consistently delivering at a high standard .

SCALING

***

If you want to scale your business, you need to be working smarter, not harder. This may mean packaging services (as discussed in the packaging chapter), bringing on team members or working '1:many' instead of '1:1'. Working '1:many' won't work for everyone, however, if you can create products or packages which can be delivered to multiple people at the same time (this is where target market is vital), you can save time, deliver more, and make more money.

Let's have a look at the team-building side of this.

Teams

Subcontracting

Subcontracting is an area that can feel exciting and scary for a business owner. Letting go and trusting someone else can be very daunting. Never forget that this fear is probably also what your client or prospect is feeling when they're considering or have hired you. It's not easy!

Many business owners are perfectionists and leaders – to let go of something and have faith that the job will still be done well, doesn't always come naturally. Add to that, the fact that you must pay someone, and it can be a most uninspiring thought indeed!

It's important to acknowledge that subcontracting and contracting aren't the same thing. Subcontracting is when we have other VAs helping us with our clients' work while contracting is when other VAs help us with our own business.

There are a couple of reasons why VAs may want to subcontract:

1. They don't have the time to do the job themselves
2. They don't want to do the job themselves
3. They can't do the job themselves.

When you decide to subcontract, you take on the role of middle-man, and you're now required to manage this project or task.

This means that you need to ensure that the communication between client and subcontractor is useful, time-efficient and productive. If you can't do this, it's best that you don't subcontract as you're just someone who is getting in the way. In this case, just direct your client to the best provider.

Knowing how you want the subcontracting arrangement to work is very important and needs to be clearly outlined in any agreement before commencement. The subcontractor is delivering a product to your client, so your reputation is on the line, and all outcomes will reflect on you and your business.

You need to be clear about what the lines of communication will be. I.e. Will the subcontractor be in direct contact with your client? Or will they need to rely on you for all direction and feedback?

Just like with working with any client or contractor, some things will always remain, such as:

1. The contractor/subcontractor needs to treat you like any other client
2. The contractor/subcontractor is delivering a service/ product to you
3. The contractor/subcontractor is responsible for managing their own time, equipment, delivery, reputation and quality.
4. You should both have clear, mutually beneficial written agreements in place.

Always have a subcontractor agreement in place before they commence work for you. The agreement needs to stipulate the same sort of things as a client agreement. It should also include the agreed forms of communication and with whom (i.e. does the subcontractor speak directly with the client, or via you?), payment terms (which may be different to a regular agreement), ownership of work, and of course, you need to stipulate the expectations around client poaching and confidentiality.

When your subcontractor or a team member communicates with any client or prospect of yours, their behaviour needs to fit within the agreement you have in place. The agreement should clearly outline whether the subcontractor or team member can offer to work directly with the prospect or client and whether they can charge directly to the client. Usually, the answer to this will be no. And there is usually an agreed period in which that restriction will remain enforced, such as 12 months. There also needs to be clear directives about what the consequences will be should those terms be breached.

They also need to work within the branding and ethical standards of your business as they are representing you. Consistency in service delivery is very important especially in the services sector, so client expectations can be set and met.

It's useful to use a project management tool when working with subcontractors. An online program which allows you to add tasks to projects and to see their status easily when your team make amendments. Whatever program you use, it needs to be easy and useful for both you and your subcontractor, so it's always used and updated.

Having clear processes and procedures in place will help ensure things are done consistently and help identify areas that need improvement.

Maintaining confidentiality is important in business and working with subcontractors is no different. Always include a confidentiality clause in your agreement and discuss how data will and can be used and shared in the team.

When it comes time to find a subcontractor, you'll no doubt be feeling like you are diving into unchartered territory. Who can you trust to help you with your clients? Who has the skills you need?

Often when VAs start looking for a subcontractor, they finally begin to realise that what they offer is unique and finding someone with the right collection of skills is not always easy. With so many different programs out there that different businesses use, it can be hard to find one person who knows the unique combination of programs that you use. You may even find that you need to give the subcontractor time to learn a new program if they're a good fit in other areas. Most VAs are very good at learning new programs which are a great asset.

Initially, you'll need to be clear on what sort of support you need. Which clients will they be helping with and which specific tasks? Make a list and start asking around your VA communities to see who has the skills and availability you need.

You'll also need to factor subcontracting into your finances. This is one of the hardest bits to start with. You want to have a margin between what you pay the subcontractor and what your client pays you. If you aren't charging enough to offer a reasonable rate to your subcontractor, you'll have issues here. You may need to increase your rates to allow for the margin, and with this increase, you need to be clear what the added benefits will be to the client. Again – you'll need amazing processes and communication in place to achieve this. Will the higher rate mean they get work done faster and more efficiently? Will it mean that there will always be someone there to help them even if a team member becomes unwell or goes on holiday? Will the extra cost to the client mean that systems are smoother and easier for them? You'll have to deliver on these!

Don't try to subcontract services that are generally charged out at a higher rate than you charge. You can't expect a VA who offers a higher-level skill to work at a lower rate than you. For higher level services you need to have a different rate to cater for the skills needed, or you can refer the client on to work directly with the specialist.

Most of the time when a VA subcontracts, they get the client to liaise through them rather than directly with the subcontractor. It is important not to do this for the sole purpose of "keeping the client" and stopping them from going off and working together with the subcontractor.

Your purpose should be to provide a more complete and holistic service to your client, allowing them one main contact person instead of having to liaise with multiple contractors. Giving them the confidence that they have a team available to them in case something goes wrong. In some cases, this process will be very easy – simply passing the job on to the subcontractor, checking it when it's returned and delivering to the client. But there may be cases where you need to step it up and take on more of a management role.

Here is a summary of some of the situations where you need to step up your involvement (or step away):

1. The client is unclear about what they want and is not sending through clear directives.

If you're passing on unclear, messy requests from the client, all you'll achieve are unclear and messy results. Your contractor may feel that their reputation is at risk as they can't deliver at the standard they would like, because the right information is not forthcoming, and they cannot speak to the client directly.

And your client will potentially waste their money.

In this situation, you need to identify (and listen if the subcontractor brings this to your attention) when directives are not clear, and the communication is going nowhere . It's your role to step in and to connect with both the client and subcontractor about what their needs are. Sometimes, especially in the case of web related work, you may need to be the 'translator' between the two. If the client is not sure what their goals are, this is when you need to decide how they can obtain clarification on goals before continuing.

2.   The job has definite timelines and other tasks associated with it that the subcontractor is not a part of.

When the job or project has more than one part, you need to manage the various elements of it if you have agreed to take on that job using subcontractors. You need to let all parties know about timelines, expectations, implications and amendments. In some cases, you also need to be the mediator, the translator or the therapist. But at the end of the day, YOU need to be delivering the product to the client.

3.   You have limited or no idea about how the service should be delivered or what information is required.

If you don't know anything about the service that the subcontractor is providing, how are you going to ensure that the service is up to standard for your client? How will you be able to assist if anything goes wrong? Will you be able to identify if there are elements crucial to the project that isn't being provided? I always recommend learning what you can about all the jobs that your subcontractors do so you can maintain quality control.

Here's an example of a recent project where I hired someone to assist me. Every time I asked a question or expressed concern, I was met with, 'I'll ask my team'. I'd then have to wait up to 12 hours for them to ask their team and get back to me, all the while hoping that they understood what my question or concern was about and that Chinese whispers weren't at play. My direct contact didn't show a strong understanding of the project or how it was being developed, and for me, this was quite frustrating.

Subcontracting is smart for business. It's important for growth. But if it were easy – everyone would be amazing at it! And everyone is most certainly not.

When you subcontract, you risk the reputation of yourself and the subcontractor. It's important to remember that when you subcontract you have still taken on the full responsibility for the delivery of the job. The buck stops with you. You can't just pass messages from party 1 to party 2 – you need to earn your piece of the pie.

Working with other VAs

VAs are awesome. I just wanted to get that out right from the start. They're usually very giving of their time, knowledgeable and keen to keep learning. They have so many great attributes. But one area that they can lack strength in is setting boundaries. Frankly, they can be too nice.

When VAs work with VAs, lines can blur very quickly. On the one hand, as a fellow VA there can be a lot of respect and mutual understanding; understanding the challenges, the juggle, and the constant evolution. But on the other hand, we can sometimes be a bit blasé about expectations, timelines and deliverables. Because, you know, they understand.

And because VAs often get along so well, they never quite get around to putting agreements and expectations in place. And those lines get blurrier and blurrier.

Here are some examples that I've seen where VAs working together hasn't worked so well.

VA takes on a subbie transcription job but doesn't confirm receipt of files or communicate about the progress of the job until it's done a few days later.

By then, the VA who needed the work done has asked someone else to help because they weren't sure that the job was in hand. The issue with this job was a lack of communication. No agreement put in place and no process expectations. Sometimes someone can take on a job, and because they are working on it, they assume all is well in the world, while the client is freaking out because they haven't been kept in the loop. A small step such as an email saying, 'File received. Will commence this evening and have finished product to you by 5pm tomorrow. Any issues and I will call you promptly. Now go and relax', would have eased the pain of the client and avoided the double up. The VA who failed to communicate receipt and progress of job would not be able to expect payment even though they may have done the job. The process and the confidence you give to the client is all part of the service.

VA works closely with a fellow VA and sends them out to meet with a prospect about a job quote. Fellow VA is asked by the prospect if they'd like to work directly with them and take out the original VA as a middle person because it's 'easier' and 'fellow VA' agrees.

No agreement was in place to prevent this, even if it's a breach of general business ethics. This issue is one that makes me cross as it was a breach of business ethics and also a friendship. It was a very strong case for agreements needing to be set up between friends as well as strangers. In this case, the VA who took on the client claimed she had done nothing wrong. There was nothing in writing to support the VA whose business the second VA was representing. Both parties seemed to have different ideas of what was ethical behaviour and what was not. Agreements must be in place and must clearly state what the expectations around the restriction of trade are.

VA starts working with another VA providing customer support but then starts to feel like they should be doing more work for the VA business and gets frustrated because they aren't getting asked to do more, and the VA business gets other VAs on board to help with specific tasks.

Sometimes when VAs work together, they can become very close. Friendship and business lines can easily become blurred, and things become awkward if you think the contractor or subcontractor isn't the right fit for a task within your business. Again, communication and planning together can help with this. The VA who owns the business has the right to work with whomever they select, and they'll usually select the person they feel is the best fit. This can be hard to stomach if you're the VA who hasn't been selected for the task. Remember that you should work in your zone of genius, and you shouldn't expect another business to hire you for a task purely because you are now friends. Hard, I know!

As you can see from the above cases, it can be very easy for lines to blur when VAs work together. VAs working together are most likely to be the ones without agreements and processes in place. Please look at what you need to do to ensure your expectations and those of your fellow VAs are clear and aligned. Things can go wrong, and it's not always where or when you expect it.

Building your team

It's not all doom and gloom – some people work fantastically together! If you consider the points above, you can set up some really strong and valuable business relationships.

Over the years I've worked alongside other VAs, coaches, designers, website developers, copywriters and bookkeepers to name a few. They've been able to help me in my business and with many of my clients. I'm great at what I do, but I don't do everything. So, to be able to provide a holistic bespoke service to my clients, I need to have people around me who can fill the gaps. And I also need to know, like and trust (that old thing again!) the people I work with.

Most of the people I've worked with over the years I've met through face to face networking or through really specialised online groups (like my Virtually Yours network) that allow you to connect with like-minded business owners. Some of my team have been working with me for upwards of 10 years. My own VA has been supporting me for many years but has stepped up to work more closely with me since my second pregnancy four years ago. It was lucky she did – I had epic baby-brain, and I had to give her tasks such as, "Remind me a week before my webinar, then remind me the day before, then remind me on the morning of my webinar, then an hour before, then five minutes before and make sure I am ON MY WEBINAR". This was because I forgot to show up for two of my webinars. Luckily, I'd also forgotten to promote them.

Some of the people I classify as 'being on my team' are people I only work with occasionally. But their input and their inspiration are invaluable, and without it, I'm not sure what I would do. Some of those people also run networks or have similar business missions to mine. I see them running their businesses and kicking goals, and I feel like together we can all achieve so much.

We all need guidance and people to inspire us and build us up. For this reason, I put an incredible value on the relationships I have with other mums in business. My best friend is also self-employed, and I met her through a 'Motivating Mum' group. This group has been wonderful and is somewhere I can brainstorm, ask the tough questions, laugh and cry. And I mean ugly-cry. I've developed some strong friendships there.

You don't always attend networking events with the intent to find a new best friend, but I did. I also found another bestie who ended up being not only one of my bridesmaids, but also my support person at the home-birth of my second child, and that was at a speed networking night! You just never know.

Other people in my team are integral in the ongoing functioning of my business. I have someone who assists with web work when I can't do it (I'm very strong in web development and can do a lot myself – but not everything), bookkeeping, accounting, and my VA is also my copywriter.

I'm also exploring the idea of working with someone on some strategic social media marketing.

I never feel alone in my business. I know who I can share what news with. I know who I can share concerns or questions with. And who I can hang out with, so I completely step away from business mode.

I see VAs working with each other, and it's beautiful. I see them building each other up, being each other's sounding boards, supporting clients together and generally being each other's rocks. I know that if one of them is unwell, the other will hold down the fort for them. I know that when one of them kicks goals, the other will be there with pom-poms akimbo. It's amazing. These VAs have something that's beneficial in business above and beyond their friendship – they know that they're not in competition and that there is enough work for us all. They have an abundance mindset, and by working collaboratively and positively, they create this abundance.

Staff members

You may find yourself wanting to hire staff rather than contractors. There are pros and cons to both types of collaboration. If you want to hire staff, you will need to work closely with your accountant to ensure you have everything in place financially. A HR expert is also someone you will need to speak to, to ensure you have the right agreements and pay rates in place.

Having staff generally means you have someone who is reliant on you for their income and they're usually only working for you. You're less likely to have staff drop off the radar or be too busy with other client work. These are problems that can arise when you hire contractors.

However, when you hire staff, you need to ensure that you are providing them with a safe environment in which to work, equipment, and entitlements as per their award wage. And of course, regular income is usually desired. You also need to be aware of their rights when it comes to leave entitlements and performance issues. You can't just fire someone because you feel like it.

If you feel you can offer this, you'll need to find the right fit just as you would when hiring a contractor. You'll no doubt find good eggs and bad eggs in your journey. That's normal!

Communication and client management steps up a notch or two when you hire staff. You need to be very clear about what their role includes, how much of their time is billable versus non-billable, what you need to be charging to ensure that their time is covered, bills are paid, and you still have an income at the end of the day. It's a big calculation process, but with the right support you can set up some good spreadsheets to ensure this is maintained.

Having project management software is vital. Programs like Asana or Teamup are great for keeping on top of who needs to be doing what and when. Team meetings need to be regular and working towards common goals will keep everyone on track.

When VAs hire staff, it's easy for them to find themselves in a position where they're not able to earn as much as before, but they're working harder. Their business turnover may skyrocket, but with staff wages and various expenses added to the fact that the VA now has to manage everyone and is working harder than ever before, means that the hourly rate of the VA can drop significantly. It's more important than ever to know your numbers, profit margins, minimum billable hours, minimum rates etc. so you don't find yourself running an empire on $5 an hour.

Myth buster: Working with other VAs can be good practice for inexperienced VAs.

BUSTED!

I'm sorry, but unless the VA that you're working with knows that you're inexperienced and you want to learn from them, any contract you agree to with another VA requires the same amount of commitment, reliability, quality, communication and service as any other client. They are a client. Any person who is paying you an amount that you have agreed to is a client. If you provide shoddy work, if you miss deadlines, if you fail to communicate – you're going to let that VA, your client, down and you're going to damage your reputation.

Working with another VA in a capacity to help you learn and grow, needs to be agreed to in separate terms. Timeframes, agreed on rates, what you're expecting from the client, and what the client is expecting from you, all need to be outlined before commencement.

If you're learning you'll probably need longer timeframes to get things done, you may need some more guidance and the client may need to allocate more time to check over your work. Your rate of pay will most likely be lower (or you may even work for free) because of this. As you learn and start delivering the service more efficiently and effectively, does the pay rate change? Does the offer of work continue? What are the expectations?

If you can't provide the service at a high and efficient standard, and you don't state this before commencement, you're not only putting your own business at risk, but you're risking that of the VA who has taken you on. In my view, this is the height of rudeness and disrespect. While I want VAs to be confident and strong in their service delivery, I also want them to be honest and clear about any shortfalls they may have. When you want to learn and grow, you need to respect the help that others will offer to you – and in return, I'm sure they will respect your desire to grow.

This can be challenging because not only can it be hard to admit you aren't great at something, but you may also come across people who would happily take advantage of this vulnerability. Some clients, for example, may offer you training and guidance in return for free or low rate work. As mentioned above, having clear timelines and expectations about this is vital. Ask them what training they'll provide in return for free or cheap work. Will you have longer timeframes to get things done? When will this 'apprentice style' of work commence and end?

You can't use clients, even if they're a VA like you, as your guinea pigs. You need always to communicate what the role is and how it will benefit both parties. It's simple really.

Managing time to maximise earning potential

Many of you won't have access to a full 5 day working week to get things done. But you probably do want to replace a full-time or part-time income.

To do this, you need to work smarter, not harder.

Consider how much money you could make if you charged hourly and you work the number of hours available to you. Deduct the amount of time you will need to spend on marketing, networking and administration, for your business – all things you cannot charge for. Consider your billable/non-billable ratio and don't assume that it will be in favour of billable! Consider the ongoing business expenses you'll need to cover. What is the most you could now earn within those constraints? For a lot of people, once they look at all these the final figures can be depressing. If it's looking good – that's awesome! Get started!

For this reason, it's worth looking at what you can offer that doesn't leave you stuck in the "billable hours" zone. It's limiting. If you can offer packages which are based on outcomes rather than hours, or you can create tools and resources which can be sold multiple times, you can find yourself working smarter, not harder.

Knowing who your ideal client is, what their pain points are and how you can ease those pain points can all significantly help when considering what packages, resources or tools to offer.

Consider if you were supporting a personal trainer who wanted to provide weekly motivational tips to her clients via SMS.

You could say to her:

"I can help you, and it will take me 2 hours per month to set those up which is $100 plus GST plus call costs."

OR you could say:

"I can source and send the motivational quotes which are on brand to your 65 members every week, allowing you to stay connected with them and provide that extra "zing" to their service. I can take this task completely off your plate for $50 per week."

The second approach looks at the results, not the time. It doesn't penalise you if you're quick and efficient at getting the job done. The factors that the client needs to consider are their member numbers, not your hours. So as their membership grows, you can requote. I'd recommend that you originally quote for a range. For example, "Send the motivational quotes to 60-70 members every week", which allows for the ebb and flow of new client numbers.

All too often business owners start their business so that they can reclaim control over their lives, their time, their choices. But without the right planning and approach, you can find yourself caught up in a business where you're working all hours of the day, too scared to take any holidays, and forgetting what your kids look like. As a prospective client, I'd be a bit concerned if someone who approached me offering to "save me time so I can do what I do best" was unable to achieve the same for themselves! Please practice what you preach and make sure you don't become a slave to your business either.

Managing time involves some key elements which I suggest you work through:

Available time

- Realistically! What time do you have available to work on and in your business? Consider your goals (below) and how much time will need to be spent ON your business rather than in it. Also consider networking events, training and education. These are all important.

- Don't forget that sometimes you'll be unproductive or perhaps be unwell or have a family member you need to look after.

Goals

(or 'desired outcomes' for the goal-phobic amongst us)

- **The big goals**: What are you trying to create? Is your business simply a job so you can earn a certain income? Is it to create a business with a team managing multiple projects? Is it to create a business that runs without you? Is it to create a business that can be sold one day?

- **The ongoing goals:** What are the things you want to achieve in your business? What are your goals and aspirations moving forward? How will these be achieved? Have you broken them down into bite-sized chunks?

- **The time goal:** What is the "time dream"? Ideally, what are the hours you want to be investing in your business on an ongoing basis?

- **The money goal:** How much money do you want to be making? Turn over? Profit? What is the financial goal?

Stakeholders

- **Support from friends/family:** This involves knowing what you want from your business and educating your friends and family so that they can support you with it. There is no point setting goals and not telling people how they need to support you to achieve them. Who is involved with helping you stay motivated? Who is helping with the kids? Who is providing feedback and advice? Who is no longer dropping in un-invited for long lazy afternoon teas during the days you want to work? Be clear about what you need from those around you and communicate it.

- **Clearly defined relationships with clients:** Clients need to be educated about how it is you need to work to achieve the best outcomes. Without clear direction, you may find clients will call you at the times that you had scheduled as "family time" or "don't disturb me I have chocolate and coffee" time. If you're unclear about your availability, you can set the relationship up for discontent and resentment. If you're clear and the client doesn't support it, then at least you know they aren't the client for you and you can move on. But without this clear communication, how can you expect them to support your plan? On a side note, make sure you know this stuff about your clients too, so you know when they're happy to be contacted and by what methods.

- **Clearly defined relationships with fellow business owners**: In a similar way to the above, the relationships you develop with fellow business owners need to be fair. You'll find that some of your new associates/friends want a lot of your time and attention, or they want your time and attention during the hours of chocolate, coffee or children (we'll call this the 3 Cs). You may also find that some of your peers/associates and yes, family/friends will want your advice or services for free. You need to have a plan about what you'll offer for free and what you won't – and stick to it. We all love to support our friends and family, but our friends and family should also be the ones supporting you by respecting your skills, knowledge and time.

No go zones

CHOCOLATE

COFFEE

CHILDREN

Tools

Using time tracking software, or software which will make you more efficient is a great idea. The software you chose will depend on the services you offer, but I recommend that you at least use something that allows you to track your contacts and what you are doing for them.

Some recommendations from existing VAs include:

- Asana
- Toggl
- My Hours
- Harvest
- Teamup
- Timestamp
- Paymo
- Trello

Outsourcing

Yep! As I always say, "Practice what you preach!". Outsource the things you aren't good at or things which are reducing your billable time or your time working on the money-making things. There are 3 reasons why VAs should be outsourcing.

Outsourcing helps you focus on:

- What you do best
- What you want to do
- What makes you money.

Outsourcing allows you to experience outsourcing for yourself. You can see what it feels like to let go (not always easy!) and what kind of service is good or bad. This is the best kind of research for your business!

Outsourcing helps you get those tasks done quicker and more efficiently.

Environment

Ensuring you have an environment which is conducive to productivity is important. Distractions are expensive! Not only do they send you crazy, but they cost you in time and energy.

Wherever it is you're working from, try to eliminate distractions such as:

- A messy desk! A clean desk does wonders for the mind.

- Noise – children (don't "eliminate" these as that's a bit extreme, but ask for help with kids if you can), building works, chatter.

- If you are someone who can't stand dirty dishes in the sink, an unmown lawn or unfolded laundry, either invest in a door or curtains or plan so that these are not an issue for you during your allocated work time. Sometimes I just spend the day working at my local café as that ticks all the boxes!

It's also useful to ensure you have access to fresh water, coffee (or hot choc as is my fuel) and a toilet is generally a pretty good idea.

Your office ergonomics need to be appropriate. Ensure you have a back-friendly chair, appropriate desk height, monitor height, no loose cables on the floor (looks at own floor in embarrassment).

Attitude

A positive can-do attitude is vital when working on your business. Any time you sit at your workstation make sure you have a focused list of things you want to work on. Tick them off as you go. Celebrate each step forward!

Sometimes you may get foggy or frustrated. Don't think that you must power through – it's a worthwhile investment to get up, walk around, pat the dog, or grab something to drink. Whatever works for you to clear the mind a bit. Your brain needs to be fueled and can't run on empty. As you work you are using your brain fuel, so don't forget to fill up now and then.

BE A 'STAND OUT' VA

***

We've explored a lot in this book. And I hope you've found some useful tips in here to help you step up towards your Stellar VA business. I wanted to give you a few extra tips to boost your results.

Things VAs do that make them less valuable

I see virtual assistants every day, both online and offline. It's my world. And I love it.

However, there are some things I see VAs doing that makes me wonder if they are self-sabotaging their success. And sometimes, it's only tiny things, but they scream "not professional enough" at me.

Here's what I've seen.

Spelling and grammar mistakes

You've probably realised that my absolute pet hate is when VAs use 'VA's' . If you're referring to a group of VAs and what they do – there is no apostrophe. And considering this is your title – it's crucial that you get this right!

Another is the misuse of words such as their, there and they're.

Here are some others I've seen that make me cringe:

- Apart versus a part
- Principle versus principal
- Stationery versus stationary
- Accept versus except
- Inquire versus enquire

I don't expect everyone to get this right all the time, but I do expect VAs to get it right when they are doing anything that represents their business.

No email signature

This one is a no-brainer. An email signature allows people to identify you and contact you quickly. Even on your mobile devices, you can set up a basic signature in your settings.

Always include your:

- Full name
- Business name
- Contact number
- Website address

- Social media links
- Logo (optional)

If you have any extra information you want to share such as hours of availability, and special promotions or encouraging people to refer their friends, pop these in too.

Underpricing services

It's important to know your value. And to be honest, many women suck at this. Channel your inner "bloke" and recognise what you're worth.

If you're secretly undercharging as you're not confident with a service, do yourself (and others who are qualified) a favour and offer something else, or get some training.

Please don't say you'll provide a service you aren't great at and justify it by offering a lower price.

Please also don't undercharge because you want to really 'wow' the client or you feel sorry for them.

Mentoring, research and training are all important - so get on it.

Being too casual too early

I love friendly, happy people. But if you're networking and you aren't confident in your brand and experience, there can be a risk of being too casual.

Yes, you can have fun and laugh – but don't get too personal too soon.

You don't know where that relationship might go, and you don't know if the person you're talking too has a similar personality that will respond well to this approach. Gauge your audience first.

Not outsourcing

Broken record here, but a VA MUST OUTSOURCE too.

You need to believe in the premise of your business – that business owners should focus on what they do best and outsource the rest.

You'll also see firsthand the restraints business owners face such as budgets and fear. Outsourcing isn't just smart for a VA – it's your research.

Using poor quality images and branding

There's simply no excuse these days to have crappy photos or images on your website and social media.

Images are affordable, and anyone can take a nice profile picture with decent lighting, doing your hair and makeup, and putting on a friendly smile.

Your brand and your image give us the first impression of how seriously you take your business. You don't have to use professional headshots (although that's ideal), but they should be bright and clean and a good reflection of your brand.

Sites like Adobe Stock allow you to purchase great images for your website and social media for reasonable prices.

Copying everyone else

It's hard to start your own thing – I know. I get it. I remember feeling so stuck trying to think of how I could make my business unique to me. I really couldn't work out what would make me different but didn't want to copy other business setups.

But that's where mentoring can be amazing and help you create something that's yours and not a duplicate of someone else's passion. You are unique, whether you realise it or not. So, embrace it and make it work for you.

If you're doing any of the above, you need to reassess and start acting, so you can fix it. If you'd like help, please contact me for a discovery session so we can nut out how you can be more professional in your business.

The VA Industry in Australia is fabulous. But it's not a cheap service, and as such, you need to step up and be amazing and show your worth.

Are you an 'opportunity radar' VA?

As a speaker, I have had many opportunities to talk to wonderful business owners about working with virtual assistants. We talk about what services VAs offer, how to plan for using a VA, so you make the most of the relationship, and the difference between onshore and offshore VAs.

As all the attendees of my presentations can attest, I always state that there are pros and cons for both onshore and offshore (offshore referring to cheaper VA options) and that when deciding which is right for them, they need to consider those pros and cons and how they impact their needs.

Of course, people talk about the price difference between Australian VAs and Filipino VAs because it's significant. A lot of admin jobs are straightforward, and someone with the right skills can do it, irrelevant of location, language or price.

But what about you? Do you consider what makes you better than the competition? Do you consider what your clients' ROI is when they work with you?

An Australian VA is a business owner who needs to find clients. You need to network and market. And you need to find solutions to a multitude of your own business needs and the needs of your clients.

This means that on your journey you should be in touch with many other business owners. And by default, this means you will be in touch with a large number of opportunities – potentially for your clients.

It is paramount that you work with your clients to identify goals and objectives. When you're networking in person or online, you need to keep an eye out for opportunities which will benefit your clients. When you're out partying, travelling, shopping or learning, you'll be able to identify opportunities for your clients once you know what it is they seek.

A good VA will know what to look for, identify opportunities and with the client, get the ball rolling. A great VA connects clients to opportunities which could impact their business success.

Don't forget that when you work with clients who you respect, you become an extension of their marketing team. When you have a great client/VA relationship, it's easy to refer clients or prospects to your client.

An Australian VA who understands business has been able to run their own business successfully for some time and who strives to keep learning and growing should always apply those same skills to their clients' business. Always look for ways to streamline their systems, improve their reach, and bring in the ideal clients. The best VAs are not just 'Online Business Managers'. The best VAs are 'opportunity radars'.

Therefore, when you say, "I'm a VA", I want you to ask yourself:

- Do I simply complete tasks?
- Do I complete the tasks and function as an "opportunity radar"?
- Do I help my clients achieve more reach, more partnerships, more connections?
- Are there opportunities in the business community that I help my clients access?

When you function as an Opportunity Radar, you can deliver more value to your ideal client. Seek clients who need what you're offering and make it easier for them to understand their ROI when they work with you.

The Virtual Assistant industry: What you can do to help it grow

I have some issues with the VA Industry in Australia as it currently stands, and I am going to lay them on the table.

VAs in Australia have a lot to contend with. For example:

- There are providers who offer the same or similar services who don't identify as Virtual Assistants (e.g. bookkeepers, graphic designers, website developers) and charge good money

- There are offshore VAs who charge $5 an hour and who are promoted by business heavyweights who seem to be keynote speakers at every second business event

- And there are VAs who are not clear about what they offer, providing every service under the sun

This is so confusing for business owners. They hear the term virtual assistant, and based on the messages out there, think 'cheap labour, low-end admin, jack of all trades master of none'. It's a huge problem for the industry.

The term 'Virtual Assistant' was coined before the internet became available to the public. It was simply offsite admin support. People used a VA for secretarial services that are easy to outsource such as typing, transcription and document formatting. Documents or 'floppy disks' were posted or physically picked up and dropped off.

A few years later, when the internet took over the world, the term was eagerly taken up by anyone offering business administrative support from an offsite location. It got even more confusing when people weren't sure if a VA was a robotic representation of someone on a website saying hello and talking to visitors, or a real contractor offering administrative support. The former seems to have died out somewhat as people focus on streamlining systems and avoiding Flash elements on their websites. Thank goodness for that.

However, over the years, the cheaper offshore business services seem to have ruled the marketing sphere for the term virtual assistant. Big business owners, mainly speakers, are heavily promoting this option and getting the word out there extremely well. And it's an option.

Meanwhile, most Australian VAs are sole traders who don't have the budget or the audience to get the message out that they even exist. And when they do manage to get out there, they seem to be saying this sort of thing:

- There are heaps of Australian VAs out there that you should hire
- Buy local and support Australian VAs
- We are better than the off-shore options.

The problem with these statements, in my opinion, is:

- Buying local isn't enough incentive for many people, especially with such a huge price difference
- Saying Australian VAs are better doesn't explain why they should be considered as an option
- Criticising the offshore options makes Aussie VAs look scared of the competition

So, I want to let you know what I think needs to change and why.

What needs to change in the VA industry

- **Standards in Australia need to be higher.** Better communication, better follow up, better training. However, to do this, VAs in Australia need to invest in their businesses and learn how to provide these services virtually in a fabulous way. Some VAs are amazing at this. I see them sucking up new knowledge and implementing it into their businesses, and they're exactly the sort of VA I'd want to work with. They take their business seriously, and they respect their clients' businesses. They think outside the square, and they find solutions. Always. They INVEST in themselves and their business. But we need more VAs to be doing this.

- **Australian VAs need to be clear about why they're worth what they're worth and communicate this well.** Your worth is not based on your country. Your worth is based on the outcomes you deliver to your clients. Your outcomes are determined by your knowledge, learning, ideas, implementation, follow up and attitude. Your knowledge, learning, ideas, implementation and attitude are determined by your experience, commitment and training.

- **Australian VAs need to identify as providers of their specific skillset.** Yes, you fit into the VA Industry; but what are you? A Social Media Strategist? Website Developer? CRM Specialist? Online Business Manager?

Bookkeeper? Copywriter? Most of these providers, when set up as contractors rather than staff, work remotely. So being virtual is part and parcel with these offerings – it's more about what the problem is that you solve rather than where you do it from. Focus on the service, not the industry title of "virtual assistant".

- **More VAs need to outsource.** VAs who fear outsourcing lose out because they:
  1. Are not practising what they preach,
  2. Can't put themselves into the shoes of their clients who HAVE outsourced and
  3. Are not able to see for themselves what works well and what doesn't. You don't run a burger shop without tasting the burgers (well not every burger, but at least one burger).

Why we need to make these changes

If we continue as we are, our industry will never grow in strength or stability. The VA industry is over 20 years old. Most people still don't know what it is or how it works .

To remain as we are, most VAs will continue to charge less than they're worth or be challenged when they do charge what they are worth.

Without a stronger industry and better understanding of their value, VAs will not be making the money they need to continue to learn what they need to learn, to be that amazing asset to their clients.

Prospects will always hear the term Virtual Assistant, and automatically rank it as a lower end administrative service that can be sourced for $5 an hour offshore.

The industry will never be able to speak as a strong force, to those in positions of power, such as government and funding bodies.

The Virtual Assistant industry in Australia is wonderful. It has incredible people within it. It also has some less than professional providers – as does every industry. It's a wonderful industry to be a part of.

But it's not a charity. It's not a hobby. It's a very, very, important income for many families, and a valuable solution for many businesses. The Virtual Assistant industry could be hugely beneficial to all Australian businesses – especially small to medium enterprises – providing growth opportunities and better work/life balance. The industry needs to take itself seriously to be heard and to grow. And now is the time.

IN CLOSING

Working within the VA Industry has been an amazing journey for me so far. Some massive highs and some terrible lows. I've seen people do wonderful things and I've seen people do unethical things that always shocked me.

The best thing has been meeting other business owners, mainly women, who create awesome businesses that are supportive and caring to their ideal client. Business owners who share and collaborate with each other, who laugh and cry together. The community spirit and the desire to keep learning and giving is what keeps me inspired.

Running your business is such a unique journey. I feel it's never possible to truly guide you with written words. It wouldn't matter how many pages this book was; I would never be able to give you every answer to every question. But I hope I can give you the feeling that you aren't alone, and that this is a wonderful industry to be a part of.

With the right thinking, every section of this book can be achieved in a fun and exciting way. Be kind to yourself. Speak kindly to yourself. Cherish the opportunities we all have to be a part of this. There are so many people who simply can't.

Please don't live to work. Please work to live. And if possible, bring your lifelong passions and drivers into your business so you can achieve more than you've ever dreamed possible.

Whenever I'm out and about on a weekday, I remember the feeling of being trapped in an office – not allowed to go out into the sunshine because I had to man the phones, or because I had to explain any reason for walking out the front door of the building – Where was I going? Why? For how long?

Now I can go where I want, when I want. And it's been 15 years since I had to explain myself. But I still make sure I remember that feeling and the resulting freedom and joy I now get from doing what I want, when I want . A sunny day, driving in the car or going for a walk – heaven. A rainy day curled up on the couch with the heater going and the laptop, a book or even a child on my lap – heaven. Days where I can power through exciting new business ideas in my home office, seeing my lovely backyard from my desk and listening to my kids playing in the next room – heaven.

Make your business work for you. For your family. Make it wonderful and shiny and desired by your ideal clients. Deliver on your promises, always be truthful and always, always, always, remember to be kind to yourself.

Love **Rosie**

INSIGHTS

From VA Superstars

The VA Industry is filled with amazing and unique people. Some of them were kind enough to tell me why they started their businesses and what keeps them going.

Often we think those things will be the same thing – but they rarely are. I love these responses below and hope you do too.

Why did they start their business and what keeps them going?

Evelyne Matti, eMatti Business Support Services

www.ematti.com.au

I started my VA business 30 years ago when my son was a toddler. I didn't want my children to be raised in daycare centres by strangers and wanted very much to be a hands-on mum with the freedom to go to school events and be able to help out when I could. It was the best decision I ever made. People tell me all the time how well-mannered my daughter and son are, and am so proud of how they have become confident, kind and well-rounded adults.

At that time, my babysitter had decided to open up a preschool and needed help setting up her branding, procedures manuals, student handbook, weekly newsletters, etc. So, I volunteered! Did it for free! Before I knew it, so many people were asking her who helped her and word of mouth spread faster than wildfire. I was working from home on a Compaq laptop, running MS DOS and 4MB RAM! No internet at that time either.

After a major hurricane destroyed the island of Kauai where we were living, my husband was transferred to South Korea where women generally could not get a work permit unless they were highly qualified in a specific field in which the country had a shortage of. Obviously, my skills were not on that 'high demand' list! So, here again, I volunteered to develop the 'Seoul Foreigners Association' operating procedures manual and helped to write the *Foreigners in Seoul Guide*, which was later taken over by the American Chamber of Commerce – it was a huge hit. I also handled a major fundraiser for the Canadian Women's Group and raised over $20,000 USD. The largest any non-profit organisation had been able to raise for local charities at the time.

We were then transferred to Thailand where I decided to complete my degree in business administration with a major in marketing, which I did online. While in Bangkok, I helped a friend set up her new art gallery and she told me "Do you know how talented you are and how many people could use your services?" ... the Internet had come of age by then, it was 1997 and I decided to set up a website, offering mostly branding and web design services at that time, thinking that so many small businesses could use a website.

We were transferred to Melbourne in 1998 and I officially registered my business in Australia and the rest is history!

What keeps me motivated?

Being able to take time off when I want to and sharing my clients' excitement when they have won a major contract or achieved a financial milestone, such as reaching their first million-dollar mark. A client recently advised me he had won a $400M contract (I had helped is team with the tender).

Now in semi-retirement, I'm happy to be able to stay home when I want to, travel when I want to, visit with grandchildren when I want to and earn pocket money to help my children and grandchildren's education fund.

I also stay motivated by keeping in touch through VYVA (Virtually Yours). I learn something new every day from the younger members and enjoy passing on my business knowledge gained from years experience in the corporate world and as a small business owner. VYVA feels like my 2nd family. To let go of VYVA would be like cutting a vital part of my life.

Rachel Boros, SB Creations

www.sbcreations.com.au

I started my VA business:

- To do the type of work I know I am good at (pick and choose, rather than go to work each day and be told what to do!)
- To be able to spend time with my kids (hypothetical kids at the time of setting up!)
- To have some control over my career

Why do I keep going?

Well, actually for a period of time I did give up! Things weren't going too well, and it all got too hard. So I went and got a part time job - which I stuck at for two and a half years even though it was boring as hell. Then one day I just had a light bulb moment where I realised the business was important to me. I did some more training, saved up our tax return money! And quit my job... and second time around things are going sooo much better!

I keep going because I love it and I can't imagine doing anything else now. And I love being a positive role model for my girls... they see Mum being the boss and working hard doing something I love. I get to do school drop offs and pick ups and volunteer at Playgroup and school etc. I keep going because I love the diversity of proof reading one day, data entry the next, social media the next and so on.

Korryn Haines, Encore Admin Consulting

www.encoreadminconsulting.com.au

I started my VA business because I grew tired of temping where I was being paid minimum wage for work that didn't utilise all of my skills for the clients I was working for.

It was by chance I met my first client who wanted me to work as a subcontractor for her because somehow she saw the potential in me and I just hit the ground running from there.

I keep going now because I can see how much my skills genuinely help my clients as small business owners and I feel like I'm actually making a significant contribution to their businesses rather than being another number in the temporary staff pool of big recruitment agencies who very often miss the mark for the kind of help businesses need.

Rachel Amies, Crazy Cat VA

www.crazycatva.com.au

Although I'm still in the start-up stages of my business, I am extremely motivated to have it succeed. Reasons that I have started the VA journey are:

- I love the idea of working from home;
- I'm tired of travelling over an hour each way, to and from a job I no longer enjoy;
- I feel undervalued and underappreciated by my employer;
- I would save travel costs and food costs by working at home; and
- I believe I can develop and increase my skillset further by working for myself.

Since starting my VA journey, I have enjoyed learning more about owning a small business. I have also been learning new skills, such as building my own website! I thoroughly enjoy the support in the Facebook VA groups I have participated in. I believe that the VA community will help keep me motivated in building and staying a virtual assistant.

Julieanne Loy, Julieanne Loy Solutions

www.julieanneloy.com.au

I started my VA business because I was in a corporate job I hated and wanted an escape.

I stay in business because it has so much more to offer, like flexibility and freedom. On days I don't feel like waking up early I don't. On days where I have no energy I rest. And I do it without guilt. I love what I do and who I work with. And now I don't think I could ever go back to having a job and working for someone else.

Stacey O'Carroll, Copperhaze VA

www.copperhazeproductions.com.au

After finishing my BA Internet Comms degree early last year I had planned to start my media company.

Partially because I wanted to be my own boss and was it bit tired of corporate. But also because I wanted to build a business that allowed me to be more creative and write more. For some reason this took a bit of time to action. I was working as a part time employee VA for a Sydney Asbestos removal company and I guess I was a little bit too comfortable.

Whilst studying my mum unfortunately was diagnosed with multiple cancers. I have spent a large amount of the past 3 years playing carer/driving on and off. Thus the flexibility that my work from home life provided became invaluable.

Fast forward to earlier this year and my part time position fell apart in tv drama style. I originally got the job through a close friend (of 20+ years), but I started to get a bit paranoid that as the company was working to move into an office that I was being pushed out. My friend started to become unavailable by email or phone for work enquiries and dismissed my concerns regarding work place harassment from another higher up employee telling me I was being paranoid. Cue mental health triggers. Things basically disintegrated over a month and I left under duress in early April, much to the disappointment of my boss. Slightly traumatic and a blow to my confidence.

Why I bring this up? The silver lining out of the drama and depression was that it allowed me time to get my ducks in a row and start to build my business. I finally had no excuses to do what I wanted.

After working as a VA I decided to make sure my business offered diverse skills and rather than just offering website management and copywriting I'd take advantage of all my previous jobs and add Virtual Assistance. I've had one client, which was from an internship I completed last year which boosted my confidence in getting things going quickly.

In regards to what keeps me going. At the moment its a giant struggle.

I underestimated how hard it would be to get my next client even though I'd heard that between the first and second client it can be quite the wait. I'm in a bit of financial stress which is making it hard to believe in myself at the moment. I had hoped at least one lead would eventuate.

But I'm frustrated and stressed. I have a mantra that I'm telling myself constantly throughout each day. Patience and persistence. I get up, check all things, post my marketing posts etc. I've found podcasts like the Socialette really helpful at the moment.

The biggest reason I keep going at the moment is I do not want to fail and I do not want to let people say that they knew I'd fail. I've had a family member suggest I go on the dole (sigh! She really doesn't understand how that works bless her). People support me but not know anyone who I can help.

I'm done with corporate, and don't want to go back to retail. I would like to prove myself that I am as talented, capable and smart as I think.

Sarah, Virtual Assistant

I had wanted to start an admin services business more than 10 years ago, but I there were too many other things going on in my life.

After my husband passed away, my priorities in life shifted. I relocated to the country in 2014 and started really wanting to kick it off, but it wasn't until 2016 that I finally bit the bullet and jumped.

The catalyst for the final leap came with my partner who suffers from chronic back pain (injuries sustained in the line of duty). The pain was causing issues with him being able to manage the business on his own. So I left my job to work part time with him and kick off my business on the side. My employer didn't want me to leave and only agreed to "let me go" if I could keep doing work for them too. So my VA business was finally born.

One of the biggest reasons for me to wanting to work independently was to escape office politics and corporate bullies. I had a nasty experience when I was working for a ruthless 'Devil wears Prada' type of woman. Even with the most recent employer the office politics was unpleasant (for different reasons).

My office is located in the back of the shop and I love working with my partner - we have such a great relationship at work and at home. The flexibility that being my own boss allows me to easily transition between roles and the ability to cover the shop if he is having a bad day. Recently I needed to go to Sydney to help with a family emergency, being able to pack up my laptop and keep working was a relief. I was able to support my family and continue with the my business no matter where I was.

My partner is selling his business now and we are relocating soon and he will probably end up working with/ for me!

123 WAYS TO USE A VA

A Virtual Assistant is someone who can assist you with business related tasks as a contractor. They work offsite and, when you hire a self-employed VA, they understand what it means to run a business.

So, you can work on what you want to work on, while the LSTs (Life Sapping Tasks) are handled by someone else!

Administration

- Internet research
- Minute taking (onsite or virtual)
- Reminder services
- Reporting
- Sourcing quotes
- Print management

Audio & video

- Editing videos / podcasts
- Editing audio files
- Recording audios
- Uploading audios / podcasts
- Uploading videos
- Audio Book publishing support

Author support

- eBook creation from existing documents
- eBook promotion
- Amazon management
- Book editing
- Publishing support

Customer services

- Answering website support tickets
- Answering website Chat enquiries
- Sending cards/gifts to clients
- Responding to email enquiries

Bookkeeping

- Bookkeeping data entry
- Invoicing

- Payment of accounts
- Debt collection

Databases

- Cleaning up, managing and updating databases
- CRM support
- Data entry

Diary management

- Appointment booking
- Booking travel, accommodation and flights
- Travel management

Documentation

- Business template creation
- File management (Dropbox, Google Drive, etc.)
- Formatting documents
- PDF conversion
- PDF creation
- Policy development and maintenance
- PowerPoint / Keynote presentations
- Preparing minutes
- Procedure development and maintenance

Email management

- MailChimp mail outs (emailers, newsletters)
- Setting up autoresponders
- Syncing calendars and making appointments
- Subscriber management

Events

- Conference registrations
- Setup of webinars
- Taking payments for events
- Webinar recording
- Booking speaking engagements
- Following up new contacts
- Event promotions
- Event follow-ups

Graphic design

- Desktop publishing
- Branding / logo design and development
- Photoshop and image editing
- Creating infographics
- Social media graphics
- Banners and signage
- Magazines

- Advertisements
- eBook and book covers

HR support and recruitment

- Real estate support
- Project management
- Mortgage broker support
- Team management
- Training

Marketing

- Blog posting
- Arranging promotions
- Arranging partnerships
- Marketing strategies
- Social media advertising

Phones

- Outbound phone calls
- Reception services
- Lead follow up

Sales

- Lead generation
- Participate in forums online on your behalf

- Follow up contacts
- Reporting

SEO support

- Directory submissions
- Tag management
- Keyword setup
- Keyword research

Social media

- Social media strategy development
- Creating and managing Facebook groups
- Managing and utilising Facebook Insights
- Creating and managing LinkedIn groups
- Creating and managing LinkedIn accounts
- Creating and managing Facebook accounts
- Creating and managing Pinterest accounts
- Creating and managing Twitter accounts
- Creating and managing YouTube accounts
- Specialty support
- Advertising strategy development

Transcription

- Legal transcription
- Medical transcription

- Focus group transcription
- Interview transcription
- Lecture Transcription
- Transcription of video and audio files
- Typing up handwritten notes
- Dictation

Websites

- eBay listings
- Filter and respond to blog / website comments
- Updating online shops
- Updating websites of all kinds
- Uploading videos to YouTube, website or other programs
- Website creation and maintenance
- Website copywriting
- Landing pages
- Setting up opt-ins
- Social media Integration
- Website security
- CRM integration

Writing

- Blog writing
- Business tender writing

- Editing
- Proofreading
- Resume writing
- Writing of emailers
- Writing of newsletters
- Writing product descriptions
- Editing and proofreading blogs
- Editing and proofreading e-newsletters
- Writing press releases
- Guest blogging / management

As you can see, many services can be provided by Virtual Assistants. As with any industry, it's important to find a VA who suits your style and your business brand. Look for VAs who are constantly working on improving their skills and services and ask your VA if they outsource any of their business tasks - it's great if they do!

A self-employed Virtual Assistant, who has been Virtually Yours "reference checked" or recommended through word of mouth is a great place to start when looking for a great VA.

If you have any questions, ask us!

VirtuallyYours®

THE VIRTUAL ASSISTANT & TRAINING NETWORK

APPENDICES

Appendix 1: Mission WOW! Client Checklist

CLIENT NAME:_____

BUSINESS NAME:_____

START DATE: _____

EXPECTED FINISH DATE:_____

ACTUAL FINISH DATE: _____

Ensure that the client is a good fit before commencing and work with them.

Make sure you are both clear on the task, the roles, and the expected outcome.

Task

_____

_____

_____

☐ Have you confirmed the task with the client?

☐ Did you paraphrase back to them to ensure you are on the same page?

☐ Have you clearly defined timelines and availability?

☐ Have you clearly outlined pricing and payment expectations?

☐ Does the client understand their role and what they need to do?

☐ Have you scheduled it into your day/week/month?

☐ Have you updated the client?

☐ Have you identified any issues and dealt with them promptly?

    ☐ If yes, did you suggest a solution(s) to your client?

    ☐ Were you able to fix the issue or work within its limits?

☐ Have you delivered on time and on budget?

☐ Has the client confirmed receipt? If not, have you followed up?

☐ Have you confirmed with the client that the service was excellent? (requested feedback on product/service)

☐ Have you asked the client if you can assist them with anything else?

☐ Have you identified any ways that the client could improve the process?

☐ Have you identified any way in which you could improve the process?

☐ Have you brought any potential improvements to the client's attention?

☐ Have you gone above and beyond for the client?

☐ Have you invoiced the client?

☐ Have you received payment?

☐ Have you connected the client to any useful resources, people or events to help

  them in their business?

☐ Have you secured additional work?

    ☐ If yes, start again!

Clients you can help

☐ Have you understood their needs?

☐ Have you provided them with some alternatives?

☐ Have you connected the client to someone who can help them?

☐ Have you followed up to make sure their needs were met?

Appendix 2: Onboarding Questionnaire #1

Courtesy Jemma Vanderboon / Your Virtual Asset

Welcome to [insert your business name]

Our aim is to be a true asset to your business, to help it grow, build and sustain momentum and in order to do this, we need to know all about it, and you!

Please fill out the following so that we can better understand your wants, needs and working style.

What is your business postal address?

_____

_____

What is your time zone? _____

What is your preferred method of communication?

_____

Email: _____

Telephone: _____

Project management software:_____

Instant messaging app (eg. Slack):_____

What is your working style? _____

Describe the days/hours your work, your working philosophies, etc.

_____

_____

Do you already have a team in place in your business? _____

Please list any specific software requirements.

_____

_____

_____

For Facebook Group support, please list Group Name below and I will request to join so that you are able to allocate me Administrator access.

_____

For Facebook Page support, please invite jemmavanderboon@gmail. com to have Administrator rights.

_____

For Email Management support, please indicate your preferred email client and any specific details you would like us to know (we will discuss this in detail before starting).

_____

If you have any documents you believe will be helpful for us in understanding your business or requirements, please share links here.

_____

_____

_____

_____

How will you determine if this project/relationship is successful?

_____

_____

_____

When is your birthday? _____

Have you worked with a virtual assistant before?

☐ Yes

☐ No

If yes, what did you like/not like about the arrangement?

_____

_____

_____

_____

Were you referred to [Insert your business name]?

☐ Yes

☐ No

If yes, who referred you (we'd like to say thank you)?

_____

_____

What can we do to 'WOW' you?

_____

_____

[Insert your business name] uses [**GSuite or Dropbox**] to share documents. If you have any documents/images that you feel will be beneficial for us in understanding your business, or that we will require to complete your tasks, please send them to: [insert your email address].

[Insert your business name] uses [**LastPass or other**] for secure password protection. Please share any passwords to [insert your email address, e.g. Gmail] (please note different LastPass email for security purposes).

I confirm that I have shared all login and password information through LastPass with [insert your email here].

☐ Yes

☐ No

Lastly, please let us know when would be a convenient time for you so we could have a chat and put together an action plan for moving forward!

Thank you! I look forward to working with you.

Appendix 3: Onboarding Questionnaire #2

Courtesy Anita Kilkenny / The Holistic VA

Hola Lovely! I know your time is precious and I'd love to start helping you as soon as possible and part of that is to ask you to quickly fill out this questionnaire which will give me an idea of your immediate and future business needs. Don't forget to save this before sending it back to me. THVA aims to provide you with solutions to your problems, save you time and oh so importantly, help grow your business.

~ Muchos gracias!

First Name:_____

Surname: _____

Company Name: _____

ABN: _____

Address: _____

_____

Email: _____

....

Phone Number(s):_____

Website : *http://_____

☐ Administrative Services

☐ Social Media Platform Set up

☐ Social Media Management

☐ nternet Marketing

☐ Event Management on and offline

☐ WordPress Maintenance

☐ Content Creation and Repurposing

☐ Desktop Publishing (e.g. eBooks)

☐ Other

If Admin Services or Other was selected, please list the specific services required.

Who is your target or niche market? Please be a specific as possible.

What are your business goals for the coming year? What do you want to blitz it at?

How are you currently supported?

☐ I am doing everything/most everything myself.

☐ I have another assistant but need more help.

☐ I have an assistant but it's not working out.

What crappy tasks are robbing you of your time?

How would you like to work? Are you driven, laid-back, organised, crazy as, etc.

Do you prefer to

☐ Email?

☐ Chat?

☐ Either?

How often do you go into melt down or have last minute tasks?

☐ All the time

☐ Sometimes

☐ Hardly ever

APPENDIX 3: ONBOARDING QUESTIONNAIRE #2

How computer savvy are you?

☐ Super savvy

☐ Somewhat savvy

☐ Not savvy at all

What software applications and platform do you use?

☐ MS Office 2010 or 365

☐ Email Marketing

☐ MAC platform

☐ MAC version of MS Office 2011

☐ Webinar/Meeting (please specify)

_____

☐ Online Bookings

☐ CRM (please specify)

_____

☐ Other specific software

_____

Please list 5 things you have been putting off and are ready to handle with my help

1._____

2._____

3._____

4._____

5._____

What is the most pressing need you have right this very second?

_____

How much are you willing to spend a month for my awesome services?

$ _____

Thank you sooo much for your time.
The answers will truly help me tailor a package for you.